PEDRO
ARRUPE

MODERN SPIRITUAL MASTERS
Robert Ellsberg, Series Editor

This series introduces the writing and vision of some of the great spiritual masters of our time. Some of these authors found a wide audience in their lifetimes. In other cases recognition has come long after their deaths. Some are rooted in long-established traditions of spirituality. Others charted new, untested paths. In each case, however, the authors in this series have engaged in a spiritual journey shaped by the influences and concerns of our age. At the dawn of a new millennium this series commends these modern spiritual masters, along with the saints and witnesses of previous centuries, as guides and companions to a new generation of seekers.

Already published:
Dietrich Bonhoeffer (edited by Robert Coles)
Simone Weil (edited by Eric O. Springsted)
Henri Nouwen (edited by Robert A. Jonas)
Pierre Teilhard de Chardin (edited by Ursula King)
Anthony de Mello (edited by William Dych, S.J.)
Charles de Foucauld (edited by Robert Ellsberg)
Oscar Romero (by Marie Dennis, Rennie Golden, and Scott Wright)
Eberhard Arnold (edited by Johann Christoph Arnold)
Thomas Merton (edited by Christine M. Bochen)
Thich Nhat Hanh (edited by Robert Ellsberg)
Rufus Jones (edited by Kerry Walters)
Mother Teresa (edited by Jean Maalouf)
Edith Stein (edited by John Sullivan, O.C.D.)
John Main (edited by Laurence Freeman)
Mohandas Gandhi (edited by John Dear)
Mother Maria Skobtsova (introduction by Jim Forest)
Evelyn Underhill (edited by Emilie Griffin)
St. Thérèse of Lisieux (edited by Mary Frohlich)
Flannery O'Connor (edited by Robert Ellsberg)
Clarence Jordan (edited by Joyce Hollyday)
G. K. Chesterton (edited by William Griffin) Alfred Delp, SJ (introduction by Thomas Merton)
Karl Rahner (edited by Philip Endean)
Sadhu Sundar Singh (edited by Charles E. Moore)

MODERN SPIRITUAL MASTERS SERIES

PEDRO ARRUPE

Essential Writings

Selected with an Introduction by

KEVIN F. BURKE, S.J.

ORBIS BOOKS

Maryknoll, New York 10545

Library of Congress Cataloging-in-Publication Data

Arrupe, Pedro, 1907-
    [Selections. English. 2004]
    Pedro Arrupe : essential writings / selected with an introduction by
Kevin F. Burke.
        p. cm. – (Modern spiritual masters series)
    ISBN 1-57075-546-9 (pbk.)
    1. Jesuits. 2. Monastic and religious life. 3. Catholic Church.
4. Theology. I. Burke, Kevin F. II. Title. III. Series.
BX3702.3.A77 2004
271′.5302 – dc22
                                                    2004009874

Contents

Sources   9

Foreword by Peter-Hans Kolvenbach, S.J.   11

Introduction
A MYSTICISM OF OPEN EYES   15

1. HIS OWN LIFE   39

Surviving the Atomic Bomb   39

Recognizing the "Hand of the Lord" at Eucharist   51

   Miracle at Lourdes   52
   Mass on Mount Fujiyama   54
   Eucharist and Solitary Confinement   55
   In the Midst of the Poor   58
   Eucharist and Hunger   59
   The Mass in "My Cathedral"   61

Fifty Years as a Jesuit   63

   Abraham, Paul, Xavier   66
   The Society, the Church, Christ   69

True Biography   73

Prayer for New Eyes   75

2. THE LIFE OF CHRISTIAN DISCIPLESHIP   76

Companions of Jesus   76

   Who Is Jesus Christ?   77
   Friends of Jesus   79

The Energy of Love   79
Following the Crucified Christ   80
Centered on Christ   81

Evangelical Poverty   82

Poverty Is a Gospel Mystery   83
Conscientization and Solidarity   86
Poverty and the Lay Christian   88

Dimensions of Christian Discipleship   90

In Service of Christ's Mission   91
Discernment   95
The Society of Jesus and the Church   98

The Sacred Heart of Jesus   101

The Word   102
The Complete Christ   103
The Humanity of Christ   105
The Divine-Human Harmonics of Love   107

Prayer to Christ Our Model   108

3. IGNATIUS LOYOLA   113

The Mystical Experiences of Ignatius Loyola   113

Ignatius's Conversion   115
Manresa   118
The Cardoner River   120
La Storta   123
Ignatius in Rome   126

The Spiritual Exercises of Ignatius   131

The Exercises and the Society of Jesus   133
Addressing the World of Today   135
Following the Pattern of Scripture   136

The Ignatian Mysticism of Love 139
    The Power of Love 140
    Love in St. Paul and St. John 140
    The Apocalyptic Finality of Love 144
An Invocation to the Trinity 148

4. THE WORLD 151
    World of Sin and Grace 151
        The Social Dimension of Sin 152
        The Eucharist and Action for Justice 154
        The Society of Jesus and Racial Discrimination 155
        The Social Commitment of the Society of Jesus 158
        On the Killing of Five Jesuits (1976–77) 160
    The Worldwide Refugee Crisis 163
        The Society of Jesus and the Refugee Problem 163
        Address to Jesuits Working with Refugees
            in Thailand 165
    Men and Women for Others 171
    Facing the World Twenty-five Years after Hiroshima 187
    Veni, Creator Spiritus 197

Epilogue
FROM SILENCE, FINAL WORDS 200
    Final Address as General of the Society of Jesus 201
    Final Homily, La Storta, Italy 203

Glossary of Ignatian and Jesuit Terms 207

Nothing is more practical than finding God, that is, than falling in love in a quite absolute, final way. What you are in love with, what seizes your imagination, will affect everything. It will decide what will get you out of bed in the morning, what you will do with your evenings, how you will spend your weekends, what you read, who you know, what breaks your heart, and what amazes you with joy and gratitude. Fall in love, stay in love, and it will decide everything.

— Attributed to Pedro Arrupe

Sources

AM   *America Magazine* 164, no. 6 (February 16, 1991)

EC   *Everybody's Challenge: Essential Documents of Jesuit Refugee Service, 1980–2000* (Rome: JRS Publications, 2000)

HA   *In Him Alone Is Our Hope* (St. Louis: Institute of Jesuit Sources, 1984)

JF   *Justice with Faith Today* (St. Louis: Institute of Jesuit Sources, 1980)

OA   *Other Apostolates Today* (St. Louis: Institute of Jesuit Sources, 1981)

OJ   *One Jesuit's Spiritual Journey: Autobiographical Conversations with Jean-Claude Dietsch, S.J.* (St. Louis: Institute of Jesuit Sources, 1986)

PH   *A Planet to Heal* (Rome: Ignatian Center of Spirituality, 1975)

RL   *Challenge to Religious Life Today* (St. Louis: Institute of Jesuit Sources, 1979)

RR   *Recollections and Reflections of Pedro Arrupe, S.J.* (Wilmington, Del.: Michael Glazier, 1986)

SL   *The Spiritual Legacy of Pedro Arrupe, S.J.* (Rome: Jesuit Curia, 1985)

Sources of Epigraphs

Collection (p. 8): Attributed to Pedro Arrupe, source unknown.

Introduction (p. 15): Ignatius Loyola, *A Pilgrim's Journey: The Autobiography of Ignatius of Loyola*, trans. Joseph N. Tylenda, S.J. (Wilmington, Del.: Michael Glazier, 1985), 38.

Introduction (p. 15): Pedro Arrupe, "The Trinitarian Inspiration of the Ignatian Charism," *The Spiritual Legacy of Pedro Arrupe, S.J.* (Rome: Jesuit Curia, 1985), 138.

Chapter 1 (p. 39): Pedro Arrupe, "Conclusion," *One Jesuit's Spiritual Journey: Autobiographical Conversations with Jean-Claude Dietsch, S.J.* (St. Louis: Institute of Jesuit Sources, 1986), 101.

Chapter 2 (p. 76): Pedro Arrupe, "Final Address of Father General to the Congregation of Procurators," *The Spiritual Legacy of Pedro Arrupe, S.J.* (Rome: Jesuit Curia, 1985), 38.

Chapter 3 (p. 113): Pedro Arrupe, "Relevance of the Society and Its Apostolate in the World of Today," *Other Apostolates Today* (St. Louis: Institute of Jesuit Sources, 1981), 16–17.

Chapter 4 (p. 151): Pedro Arrupe, "Witnessing to Justice in the World," *Justice with Faith Today* (St. Louis: Institute of Jesuit Sources, 1980), 83.

Epilogue (p. 200): Ignatius Loyola, *The Spiritual Exercises of Saint Ignatius,* #234, trans. and ed. G. Ganss (St. Louis: Institute of Jesuit Sources, 1992).

Foreword

This collection of writings gives clear evidence that Pedro Arrupe is a contemporary spiritual master. But it is important to understand this title correctly. In John the Baptist, that great ascetic, prophet, forerunner, and witness, we encounter a disposition that is fundamental to the Christian understanding of a *spiritual master.* John says that Jesus is "the one who comes after me but ranks ahead of me" (John 1:30). He gives witness to Jesus as "the Lamb of God" and, when two of his disciples hear this, they leave him and follow Jesus (John 1:35–36). Likewise, in a moving passage often referred to as John's "final testimony," he speaks with great love and freedom about his relationship to Jesus and the fulfillment of his own ministry:

> The one who has the bride is the bridegroom; the best man, who stands and listens for him, rejoices greatly at the bridegroom's voice. So this joy of mine has been made complete. He must increase; I must decrease.
>
> (John 3:29–30)

Pedro Arrupe is a spiritual master in the line of John the Baptist. Like John, he speaks prophetically from a life of ascetical simplicity and compassion. He confronts the great ethical and religious questions of the day, challenging not only his brother Jesuits and other men and women in vowed religious life, but all Christians and all people, to be rooted in truth and guided by love. He calls for authentic spiritual renewal, integrating prayer with the life of service. But above all, Father Arrupe is profoundly and passionately committed to Jesus Christ. Like John, he draws attention away from himself to Christ. He makes John's words his own: *he must increase; I must decrease.* Just so, the point of this book is not to draw attention to Pedro Arrupe. Rather, it calls us to look where Don Pedro is pointing, to see the world and the church as he saw them and, in everything, to see Jesus and hear his call.

Of course, Pedro Arrupe must also be viewed as a spiritual master in the line of St. Ignatius Loyola, the "father in faith" of every Jesuit. St. Ignatius, the founder and first Superior General of the Society of Jesus, nurtured his new order during the tumultuous years of the Reformation and the Council of Trent. Similarly, as the Jesuit General from 1965 until 1983, Father Arrupe led his brother Jesuits through a challenging period of renewal called for by the Second Vatican Council. As Ignatius showed a special love for the poor, Don Pedro drew attention to the plight of the suffering, especially refugees and the victims of war and violence. Father Arrupe also manifests Ignatius's great love for the church, promoting its teachings, including its understanding of the inseparable connection between faith and justice. Indeed, Ignatius Loyola and Pedro Arrupe shared the same mysticism, the graceful familiarity with God grounded in the Spiritual Exercises that Ignatius crafted and that Don Pedro revitalized. Thus, throughout his life and especially in his final years, Father Arrupe made the prayer of St. Ignatius from the Spiritual Exercises his own:

> Take, O Lord, and receive all my liberty, my memory, my understanding, and my whole will. All I have and all I possess are yours, Lord. You gave them to me, and I return them to you. Dispose of them as you will. Give me your love and your grace, and I shall want for nothing more.

In this book we read the words of Father Pedro Arrupe, but find far more than his words. We find his faith, his love, his life.

This is what matters, for as Don Pedro himself said, "Nowadays the world does not need words, but lives which cannot be explained except through faith and love for Christ poor." Pedro Arrupe loved the poor Christ and Christ in the poor. In so doing he earned a place of respect and love in the hearts of his brother Jesuits. But he no longer belongs to Jesuits only. Like Ignatius and like John the Baptist, he belongs to the whole church. Indeed, he belongs to the whole world.

PETER-HANS KOLVENBACH, S.J.
Superior General of the Society of Jesus
July 31, 2004

Introduction

A Mysticism of Open Eyes

As he sat there the eyes of his understanding were opened
and though he saw no vision he understood and perceived
many things.   —*Ignatius Loyola*

Grant me, O Lord, to see everything now with new eyes.
...Give me the clarity of understanding that you gave
Ignatius.   —*Pedro Arrupe*

The life of Pedro Arrupe stretched over most of the twentieth
century, touching all of its decades. He lived through a time
when massive historical changes rocked the Catholic Church
and the world at large. In the church, the Second Vatican Council (1962–65) ignited an extraordinary process of renovation
in response to the signs of the times. The church dramatically
adapted its liturgies and devotions, and significantly deepened
its theological self-understanding. It renewed the forms of religious life and rediscovered the role of the laity. It shifted its
relationships with other churches and other religions, and re-
defined its relationship to secular institutions and to the world
itself as "secular." Meanwhile, dizzying changes also affected
the larger secular world. After the First World War derailed the
runaway train of a prevailing post-Enlightenment optimism, the
Second World War exposed the savage darkness of a shattered
world. From the demonic nightmare of the Shoah and the destructive rage of the atomic bomb, Auschwitz and Hiroshima
emerged as stark icons of a new era. The Cold War assumed

center stage, with the nuclear superpowers establishing a precarious balance of terror upon the threat of mutually assured destruction. Countless regional wars and revolutions broke out, along with vicious episodes of genocide, ethnic cleansing, planned famines, and forced migrations. The century witnessed the rise and fall of new political and economic powers, and the displacements of whole populations. It was a century of violent excesses and apocalyptic ruptures.

The bloodiest century in recorded history now recedes from view. It seems a time of unending tragedy. Yet, for all its darkness and horror, it was also a century of unexpected light and grace. Alongside its dictators and tyrants, it produced women and men of extraordinary holiness and deep humanity, courageous prophets and geniuses of the spiritual life. Mohandas Gandhi, Etty Hillesum, Alfred Delp, Thomas Merton, Martin Luther King, Dorothy Day, Karl Rahner, Oscar Romero, and many others. Amid the company of these spiritual giants we also find the fiery but humble Basque Jesuit, Pedro Arrupe.

Born in Bilbao, Spain, on November 14, 1907, Arrupe entered the Society of Jesus at the age of nineteen. In 1965, just before Vatican II reached its momentous conclusion, he was elected Superior General of the Jesuits. He died in Rome on February 5, 1991, as the Cold War was ending, nearly ten years after suffering a debilitating stroke that led to his retirement in 1983. Between his obscure beginning and silent ending, during the years of his formation as a student of medicine, philosophy, psychiatry, theology, and the spiritual life, and all through his years of active ministry as a priest, missionary to Japan, novice master, provincial superior, and, finally, the leader of the largest and most influential religious order in the Catholic Church, Arrupe lived with passion and optimism amid the tragedies of his world and the monumental changes occurring in his church. He was a contemplative: a man of deep prayer, religious devotion, and spiritual discipline. At the same time, he led an active life of service as an administrator, teacher, writer, public speaker, and priest. From the heart of this life of contemplation and action he produced a masterful interpretation of Christian spirituality and the challenges of Christian discipleship. His writings merit careful reflection.

However, Arrupe's writings are not easy to systematize or absorb. For one thing, they are voluminous. A least nine collections of essays, instructions, letters, informal talks, formal addresses, homilies, interviews, and memoirs have appeared in English, and this represents only a fraction of the material contained in Jesuit archives around the world.[1] But even with the material more or less accessible in English, some difficulties appear for the general reader today. Many of Arrupe's official letters to the Society of Jesus, as well as his talks addressed to religious orders and lay associations, reflect the peculiarities of intraecclesial concerns and the specific exigencies of a time already fading into the past. Moreover, they often employ an "insider's vocabulary" and assume a set of references with which most people are not acquainted. He draws on patristic and medieval categories in his homilies, admonitions, and essays, thus presuming a somewhat advanced theological literacy.

---

1. See Pedro Arrupe, *A Planet to Heal: Reflections and Forecasts* (Rome: Ignatian Center of Spirituality, 1975); *Challenge to Religious Life Today: Selected Letters and Addresses I* (St. Louis: Institute of Jesuit Sources, 1979); *Justice with Faith Today: Selected Letters and Addresses II* (St. Louis: Institute of Jesuit Sources, 1980); *Other Apostolates Today: Selected Letters and Addresses III* (St. Louis: Institute of Jesuit Sources, 1981); *On Spirituality for Today's Jesuits: Five Recent Documents from Fr. General Pedro Arrupe, S.J.* (St. Louis: Institute of Jesuit Sources, 1980); *In Him Alone Is Our Hope: Texts on the Heart of Christ* (St. Louis: Institute of Jesuit Sources, 1984); *The Spiritual Legacy of Pedro Arrupe, S.J.* (Rome: Jesuit Curia, 1985); *Recollections and Reflections of Pedro Arrupe, S.J.* (Wilmington, Del.: Michael Glazier, 1986); *One Jesuit's Spiritual Journey: Autobiographical Conversations with Jean-Claude Dietsch, S.J.* (St. Louis: Institute of Jesuit Sources, 1986).

His letters and addresses on Christian discipleship make fre-
quent allusions to the story and practice of Ignatius Loyola, the
founder and first Superior General of the Jesuits; they can be
hard to follow for readers unfamiliar with the life of Ignatius
and the Ignatian Spiritual Exercises.

Attentive to these difficulties, the present collection — *Pedro
Arrupe: Essential Writings* — has a simple aim: to make Arrupe
accessible to a general audience. The selections contained here
represent — or at least may represent — "essential writings"
in two different senses. First, they provide new readers with a
taste of the "essence" of Arrupe's spiritual vision. Second, and
more importantly, they may prove "essential" for those who
are restless with spiritual hunger, especially those who feel compelled to correlate transcendence and history precisely because
their attraction to mysticism arises from a deep passion for this
world. Arrupe's reflections speak to such hungers and passions,
for they emerge from the heart of a man who knew intimately
the Spirit and the world. Poignant and at times personal, these
recollections, essays and prayers reveal a man whose familiarity with suffering and long apprenticeship in the art of spiritual
conversation rendered him finally, simply human. More to the
point, these words spring from the vision of a mystic, but a
very particular kind of mystic: one who epitomizes what Johann
Baptist Metz tellingly calls "a mysticism of open or opened
eyes."[2]

With this bold image in mind, and in an effort to place
Arrupe's writings in context, I divide the remainder of these
introductory remarks into two main parts. First, I sketch Arrupe's life, assessing his legacy while highlighting key influences,
turning points, and accomplishments. Second, with reference to

---

2. Johann Baptist Metz, *A Passion for God: The Mystical-Political Dimension
of Christianity*, trans. J. Matthew Ashley (New York and Mahwah, N.J.: Paulist
Press, 1998), 163.

St. Ignatius I probe the mysticism of open eyes by which Arrupe thoroughly embraced the good of this world and its transcendence. I conclude with a few notes about the way I arranged and edited the selections included in this book.

The Life of Pedro Arrupe

Pedro Arrupe grew up in a caring family of modest means, the youngest child and only boy among five children. He lost his mother when he was ten years old and his father when he was eighteen. At the age of fifteen, having completed his secondary education, he began undergraduate studies in medicine at the University of Madrid. In 1926, after the death of his father, he and his sisters traveled to Lourdes, where he offered his services as a doctor to the Medical Verification Bureau. In that capacity he witnessed several miraculous healings (see below, p. 52), an experience that led him eventually to set aside his medical career and enter the Society of Jesus on January 15, 1927.

In 1932 the Spanish Republic expelled all the Jesuits from the country. Engaged in philosophy studies at the time, Arrupe went into exile in Marneffe, Belgium. The following year he was sent to Valkenburg, Holland, to undertake advanced studies in theology and medical ethics. He was ordained to the priesthood on July 30, 1936, and then spent several months conducting research in psychiatry in Washington, D.C., before completing a fourth year of theology at St. Mary's, Kansas, and his final year of religious training (tertianship) in Cleveland, Ohio. In 1938 he received word from Rome that after years of persistent pleading his request to be a missionary had been granted.

On the eve of the Second World War Arrupe traveled from the United States to Japan to begin learning a new language in preparation for a life of missionary work among the Japanese people. This period of his life included moments of suffering as well as mystical consolations, both of which appear in his eucharistic recollections: the spiritual joy of celebrating mass on the summit of Mount Fuji at daybreak; the spiritual suffering of being deprived of the Eucharist for thirty-three days while held in solitary confinement by the Japanese government, which suspected him of espionage (see below, pp. 54–58). Shortly after he was released from prison in 1942, Arrupe was sent to Nagatsuka just outside of Hiroshima to assume the position of master of novices. He was in the novitiate building on the morning of August 6, 1945, when the first atomic bomb incinerated the city of Hiroshima. Arrupe, the novice master, once again took up the profession of medicine, converting the novitiate into a makeshift hospital and caring for over 150 people suffering from the mysterious aftereffects of radiation poisoning. In the years following the war he traveled around the globe recollecting what he experienced and examining what it revealed about our world (see below, pp. 39 and 187). He indicated that the apocalypse of Hiroshima changed his life. It deepened his sense of dependence on God and opened his eyes to "what is deadly and truly terrible about force and violence" (see below, p. 196).

In 1954 Arrupe was appointed superior of the two hundred Jesuits working in the vice-province of Japan. Eventually the vice-province grew into a self-sustaining province, and in 1958 he was named its first provincial. When the Superior General of the Jesuits, Jean-Baptiste Janssens, died in October 1964, Arrupe went to Rome as a delegate to the Thirty-first General Congregation (GC 31), which met to elect a successor. On the morning of May 22, 1965, much to Arrupe's surprise, the Congregation elected him. As an immediate consequence of his election, he received an invitation to participate in the final session of Vatican II. He offered input during the debate on the Council's final document, the "Pastoral Constitution on the

Church in the Modern World" (*Gaudium et spes*), commenting on the crucial task of inculturation.

As the Superior General of the Jesuits during the period of renewal following Vatican II, Arrupe embodied a view of religious leadership rooted in collegiality, discernment, and service. He promoted the thoroughgoing renovation of the Society of Jesus, as the conciliar decree on religious life mandated, and his immediate impact on Jesuit religious life has been viewed as nothing short of a refounding of the order. But his influence did not stop there. He was elected the president of the Union of Religious Superiors General in 1967 and held the position for five consecutive terms until 1982. As a result he attended bishops' meetings and synods, providing commentary and advice mined from the collective wisdom of various religious congregations. He also visited different religious communities and urged them to respond to Vatican II and the needs of the world with courage, generosity, and hope. By his example he showed what fruit might spring from the cultivation of these virtues.

Beyond the ambit of religious life, Arrupe is recognized for the influence he exercised in the church and the world. Moved by an intense, lifelong fidelity to the church and a deep personal loyalty to the Holy Father, he became a major commentator on and promoter of the decrees of the Council, and drew attention to issues of war and peace, poverty and development, and other matters of social concern addressed in later papal encyclicals. The corpus of his writings witnesses to his talent for reconciling seeming opposites: the old and the new, tradition and renovation, freedom and obedience, religious devotions and secular politics, centers of power and the world's margins, and so on. Over and over, one encounters in Arrupe an unflagging optimism rooted in faith and a penetrating grasp of the logic of evil so pervasive in our world. Over and over one meets in him a man of prayer engaging the world, a man who could "find

God in all things," as St. Ignatius would have it. Over and over one sees that just as Arrupe loved his own family, close friends, and brother Jesuits, he spent himself reaching out to unknown others, above all those who were suffering: the ravaged survivors of the atomic bomb (see below, p. 39), victims of racism (p. 155), hunger (p. 154), political exploitation, economic displacement, and marginalization (p. 86), the masses of poor people scratching out an existence on tiny impoverished farms or in the squalid urban slums of the world (p. 58), and, in a particularly urgent way, the "boat people" and other refugees (p. 163).

Arrupe's personal concern for the poor and his visionary reading of the church's social gospel fed his concern to renew the vitality of Christian discipleship around the intrinsic connection between faith and justice. This became the defining mark of his years as the General of the Society of Jesus. In the period following Vatican II the church dramatically advanced its social teachings. In 1967 Pope Paul VI issued *Populorum progressio,* an important encyclical that analyzes and addresses the social and political realities of the modern world in the light of the Gospel. The following year the Latin American Bishops' Conference held a meeting in Medellín, Colombia, which interpreted Vatican II through the lens of Latin America's staggering poverty and political oppression. Medellín proved to be a watershed in the recent history of the continent. Among other things, this shifted the church's self-understanding and pastoral priorities, and facilitated the emergence of basic ecclesial communities. Arrupe was deeply involved in these events. He not only attended the Medellín conference but, through his admonitions and encouragement to Jesuit pastoral workers, theologians, and provincials, he provided crucial support to the implementation of the Medellín documents and the growth of liberation theology.[3] In 1971, the Synod of Bishops issued its seminal document, *Justice in the World,* and the following year Arrupe wrote a lengthy commentary, which was published by the Pontifical Commission on Justice and Peace (excerpts of his commentary can be found below, pp. 86 and 95). Around this time Arrupe also delivered a controversial and widely discussed address to the alumni of Jesuit high schools, the title of which was subsequently adopted as the unofficial motto of many Jesuit institutions: "Men and Women for Others" (see below, p. 171).

In 1973, having judged that the time was ripe for an in-depth assessment of the Society's response to Vatican II and its mission in the world, Arrupe called the Thirty-second General Congregation (GC 32).[4] In so doing he inaugurated the most important event of his tenure as Superior General of the Society of Jesus. Along with GC 31 (over which he also presided after his election as Superior General), GC 32 is widely recognized as one of the most important Congregations in the history of the order. Moreover, with good reason it has been frequently called "Arrupe's Congregation." He did not micromanage the Congregation, nor did he personally author its decrees. But it reflected his collegial style of leadership, his capacity to trust God's spirit, and his willingness to be guided and informed by others, including his brother Jesuits, the Holy Father, and, above all, the concrete needs of the church and the world. His distinctive stamp can be felt within and throughout the documents of the Congregation, and nowhere more clearly than in the signature passage from the decree entitled "Jesuits Today."

---

3. See Christian Smith, *The Emergence of Liberation Theology: Radical Religion and Social Movement Theory* (Chicago: University of Chicago Press, 1991), 132–34.

4. General Congregations represent the highest authority in the Society of Jesus. Besides electing new Generals when necessary, they establish priorities for the Society's mission, ministries, and community life.

What is it to be a companion of Jesus today? It is to
engage, under the standard of the Cross, in the crucial
struggle of our time: the struggle for faith and that struggle
for justice which it includes.[5]

Arrupe is not the first to speak about a "faith that does justice,"
nor can he be credited with formulating the practical mysticism
that seeks to integrate the struggle for faith and the struggle
for justice. But the adoption of this stance by GC 32 exerted a
profound impact on the Society of Jesus and all its institutions,
to say nothing about religious life in general and the larger
church — an impact that owes much to Arrupe's leadership.

In the years following GC 32, in addition to the important work of encouraging the worldwide Society of Jesus to
implement its decrees, Arrupe turned increased attention to
the dynamics of Ignatian spirituality. Over a period of several
years he conducted courses at the Ignatian Center of Spirituality in Rome. On the basis of those courses he wrote three
of his most important essays on the mysticism of Ignatius and
the charism of the Society of Jesus: "Our Way of Proceeding"
(1979, pp. 81, 108, 138); "The Trinitarian Inspiration of the Ignatian Charism" (1980, pp. 118–126, 139); and "Rooted and
Grounded in Love" (1981, pp. 126–131; 136–137; 140–148).[6]
Between Christmas of 1980 and Easter of 1981, Arrupe also
agreed to give an extended interview to a French Jesuit, Jean-
Claude Dietsch. While not a full autobiography, this short book

---

5. Society of Jesus, General Congregation Thirty-two, Decree 4, "Our Mission
Today," in Documents of the 31st and 32nd General Congregations of the Society
of Jesus (St. Louis: Institute of Jesuit Sources, 1977), 401.

6. These three essays can be found in The Spiritual Legacy of Pedro Arrupe, S.J.
(Rome: Jesuit Curia, 1985). In addition, the first two are reprinted in On Spiritu-
ality for Today's Jesuits: Five Recent Documents from Fr. General Pedro Arrupe,
S.J. (St. Louis: Institute of Jesuit Sources, 1980), 35–66, 67–111. "Rooted and
Grounded in Love" appears in One Jesuit's Spiritual Journey (St. Louis: Institute
of Jesuit Sources, 1986), 105–60.

does provide a sketch of his religious vision, and an intimate portrait of his gracious, humorous and humble manner.[7]

In early September 1981 Arrupe followed up an exhausting two-week visit to the Philippines with a brief stop in Thailand to visit the refugee work of the Jesuits there. Just a year after founding Jesuit Refugee Services, Arrupe took this occasion to praise the efforts of the refugee workers. Near the end of his remarks, he exhorted them:

> I will say one more thing and please don't forget it. Pray. Pray much. Problems such as these are not solved by human efforts. I am telling you things that I want to emphasize, a message — perhaps my "swan song" — for the Society (p. 171).

Indeed this was Arrupe's "swan song." On his arrival at the airport in Rome the following morning, September 7, 1981, he suffered a massive stroke from which he would never fully recover. His speech center was severely impaired and he remained partially paralyzed for the rest of his life. Just months before, aware of his growing age and infirmity, he had attempted to resign as General, but Pope John Paul II had denied his request. Once it became clear that the stroke was of such a severity that Arrupe could not continue his duties, the pope intervened in the Society's normal procedures for succession. He removed Arrupe's General Assistant, Father Vincent O'Keefe, and appointed as his own delegate an elderly Italian Jesuit, Father Pablo Dezza, to head up the Society indefinitely. Overcome with grief when he learned of this extraordinary intervention into the governance of the Society, Arrupe burst into tears. He was

---

7. Arrupe, *One Jesuit's Spiritual Journey.* An interesting parallel emerges with Ignatius, who dictated his spiritual autobiography late in his life at the insistence of several of his closest advisors; see Ignatius Loyola, *A Pilgrim's Journey: The Autobiography of Ignatius of Loyola,* trans. Joseph N. Tylenda, S.J. (Wilmington, Del.: Michael Glazier, 1985).

embarking on the most difficult decade in his life, a decade of forced inactivity and silence, a season of profound spiritual poverty and surrender. Yet he met these challenges with courage and trust in God. When General Congregation Thirty-three (GC 33) was eventually convoked in September 1983, Arrupe was able to attend its opening session and formally resign as General of the Society of Jesus. Because of the effects of the stroke he could not speak directly to his brother Jesuits, but his final address was read to them in his presence (p. 201). Similarly, his final homily was delivered on his behalf at mass the following day in the famous chapel of La Storta (p. 203). His trust in God remains his most enduring legacy.

> A profound experience of the loving protection of divine providence has been my strength in bearing the burden of my responsibilities and facing the challenges of our day. True, I have had my difficulties, both big and small. But never has God failed to stand by me. And now more than ever I find myself in the hands of this God who has taken hold of me. (See below, p. 204)

The Ignatian Roots of Arrupe's Mysticism

How did Pedro Arrupe come to speak this way? What spiritual experiences planted and nourished his confidence in God? And what can we learn from him? What gift does he offer us today? What word of hope in response to our most urgent longings?

I have referred to Arrupe as a mystic, but this designation can be highly misleading. For one thing, he never used this category to speak of himself or his own experiences in prayer. He refused to be drawn into a cult of personality, because he understood too well the dangers of spiritual pride. He also knew that labels like mystic, guru, holy man, or saint are often used to pigeonhole people of faith, to domesticate their words by creating a distance between their example and the lives of "ordinary people." For another thing, Arrupe really did not see himself as special, as the selections below reveal. While he did speak openly about the graces he received during his lifetime, whenever he himself became the focus of conversation, he drew attention precisely to his ordinariness and above all to his faults, failures, and sins. Like all true spiritual giants, he seemed unaware of his distinctive spiritual gifts. He considered himself a simple man utterly bereft but for the grace of God. Speaking of such souls, the poet Denise Levertov observes:

> They know of themselves nothing different
> from anyone else. This great unknowing
> is part of their holiness. They are always trying
> to share out joy as if it were cake or water,
> something ordinary, not rare at all.[8]

Understanding Arrupe as a mystic runs into a further problem, one created by the tendency to overidentify mystical experience with miraculous visions, spectacular interior dramas, and otherworldly transports. Not every mystical experience involves visions per se and not every mystic withdraws from the world. Arrupe's life manifests the practical, apostolically oriented mysticism that flows from St. Ignatius's Spiritual Exercises. Likewise, his spiritual life assumed the contours of Ignatius's mystical itinerary. As a way of elaborating this latter point, I draw attention to several key moments in the life of Ignatius and Arrupe's reflections on them.

Like Arrupe, Ignatius Loyola lived during a time of social upheaval and massive cultural transformation. He was born in

---

8. Denise Levertov, "Translucence," in *This Great Unknowing: Last Poems* (New York: New Directions, 1999), 48.

1491 in the Basque region of northern Spain and died in Rome in 1556. He thus lived through the early stages of the Protestant Reformation and the conquest of the Americas. This was the age of the printing press and the earliest recorded circumnavigations of the globe, the dawn of the modern era. All of this affected Ignatius, but he was marked at least as much by the piety and structures of medieval courtly life, and his own early training as a courtier and a knight. The turning point in his life occurred in battle in 1521 while defending a fortress near the town of Pamplona. A cannon ball shattered his leg, and during his excruciating convalescence, he began to notice within himself the movements of different spirits and a desire to go on pilgrimage to Jerusalem once he had recovered his strength (p. 115).

The first part of Ignatius's pilgrimage led him to the town of Manresa, where he withdrew to a cave and lived a life of extreme austerity for the better part of a year (p. 118). As his interior movements grew in intensity, he engaged in a range of "spiritual exercises," including fasting, examining his conscience, going to confession, and meditating on the Gospels. These experiences in prayer formed the basis of a spiritual program focusing on conversion and discernment that eventually grew into his most important written work, *Spiritual Exercises*.[9] In his autobiography, Ignatius attests that the main actor in the drama that unfolded in Manresa was God. Moreover, he experienced God as his teacher. "During this period God was

---

9. Ignatius Loyola, *The Spiritual Exercises of Saint Ignatius*, trans. and ed. G. Ganss (St. Louis: Institute of Jesuit Sources, 1992). The *Spiritual Exercises* provides a detailed method for the practice of a spirituality of discipleship rooted in the Gospels. It attempts not to describe but to facilitate an encounter with God, and to draw one into a living experience of God's presence and action. In order to distinguish the written text of the *Spiritual Exercises* from the act of doing the Spiritual Exercises (or directing another who is doing them), the former appears in italics and the latter does not. (For Arrupe's reflections on the Ignatian Exercises, see below pp. 133–139).

dealing with him in the same way a schoolteacher deals with a child while instructing him."[10]

At Manresa, Ignatius experienced the most dramatic interior lesson of his life. It happened one day while he was meditating near the banks of the Cardoner River (see p. 120).

> As he sat there the eyes of his understanding were opened and though he saw no vision he understood and perceived many things, numerous spiritual things as well as matters touching on faith and learning, and this was with an elucidation so bright that all these things seemed new to him.[11]

Ignatius goes on to comment that he learned more on that one occasion than in all the other experiences of his life added together. The experience involved a kind of "seeing," though not in the sense of ocular vision. It was a spiritual illumination — the opening of "the eyes of his understanding." This was the grace that Arrupe sought when he prayed: "Grant me, O Lord, to see everything now with new eyes.... Give me the clarity of understanding that you gave Ignatius." In his essay on the trinitarian logic of Ignatius's mysticism, he offers further commentary on the essence of this grace.

> It is an infused intellectual illumination about the divine essence and the Trinity of Persons in a generic way and, more concretely, about two of its outwardly directed operations: the creation and the incarnation. Ignatius is brought into the *trinitarian* intimacy and finds himself an illumined spectator of the creation and incarnation in a trinitarian context. (See p. 122)

---

10. *A Pilgrim's Journey,* 35–36.
11. *A Pilgrim's Journey,* 39. Arrupe quotes this passage in his essay "The Trinitarian Inspiration of the Ignatian Charism" (see below, p. 120). Note that Tylenda's translation cited here differs from the translation used in the official English text of Arrupe's essay cited below.

Ignatius experienced many other mystical graces, but alongside the illumination at the Cardoner River, one in particular stands out: his vision in the chapel at La Storta while on his way to Rome in 1537 with Diego Laínez and Pierre Favre. To this momentous event he dedicates only a one-sentence description in his autobiography. "One day, a few miles before reaching Rome, while praying in a church, he felt a great change in his soul and so clearly did he see God the Father place him with Christ, his Son, that he had no doubts that God the Father did place him with his Son."[12] Although Ignatius gives us but the bare outlines of his vision, his companions later supplied a fuller picture of it.

> As Ignatius entered the chapel he felt a sudden change come over him, and while he was praying he had a remarkable vision. He saw God the Father together with Jesus, who was carrying his cross. Both Father and Son were looking most kindly upon him and he heard the Father say to the Son: "I want you to take him as your servant." Jesus then directed his words to the kneeling pilgrim and said: "I want you to be our servant." This was exactly what Ignatius had always wanted. Then he heard the Father add: "I will be favorable to you in Rome." This was God's answer to Ignatius's frequent prayer that he be placed next to Mary's Son. Leaving the chapel and continuing his way to Rome, Ignatius did not know whether he would meet success or persecution, but he knew that God would be with him.[13]

---

12. *A Pilgrim's Journey*, 113.

13. Joseph Tylenda, "Commentary," in *A Pilgrim's Journey*, 113. Tylenda draws on the testimony of Diego Laínez; see *Monumenta Historica Societatis Iesu*, vol. 73 (Madrid and Rome, 1951), 133. For Arrupe's commentary, see below, p. 123. See also p. 204.

Arrupe, in line with the biographers of Ignatius and the leading historians of the Society of Jesus, focuses on the essential point of the vision. "Ignatius, creator of this apostolic group and bearer of the virtual charism of the Society whose existence is assured at that very moment, is received as the servant of Jesus and of the Father in Jesus" (see below, p. 124). La Storta is the summit of Ignatius's mystical experiences. It links the life-changing illumination of the Cardoner to his life's vocation. He is called to be a companion of Jesus carrying his cross. Within two years of La Storta, Ignatius and his first companions begin a new religious order. Because of the inspiration of La Storta, Ignatius will insist that this new society take the name of Jesus. The vision at La Storta thus links the mysticism of Ignatius to the essential charism of the Society of Jesus. Not surprisingly, both Arrupe and GC 32 find in La Storta the touchstone of the Society's renewal as an apostolic order. The latter expresses this succinctly.

> What is it to be a Jesuit? It is to know that one is a sinner, yet called to be a companion of Jesus as Ignatius was: Ignatius, who begged the Blessed Virgin to "Place him with her Son," and who then saw the Father himself ask Jesus, carrying his Cross, to take this pilgrim into his company.[14]

The heart of Ignatian spirituality — the spirituality that so deeply formed Pedro Arrupe — appears between the poles of these two great mystical experiences in the life of Ignatius. The Cardoner generates the spiritual program of conversion, discernment, and vocation outlined in the *Spiritual Exercises*. La Storta further specifies the content of this conversion, discernment, and vocation in the lives of Ignatius and his companions. Theirs is an apostolic life focused on mission and praxis, a

---

14. "Jesuits Today," 401.

mysticism of discipleship that follows Jesus carrying his cross, a spirituality of service with a particular sensitivity for suffering. This spirituality appears in historical continuity with the mysticism of St. Francis of Assisi, one of Ignatius's spiritual heroes. A contemporary historian of spirituality, Ewert Cousins, refers to this broad Franciscan-Ignatian current in the history of Christian spirituality as a "mysticism of the historical event." Cousins writes, "Just as in nature mysticism we feel united to the material world, so in this form of mysticism we feel part of the historical event — as if we were there, as eyewitnesses, participating in the action, absorbing its energy."[15] The movement into historical events that we see in Francis's erection of the Christmas crèche or his desire to imitate and follow the poor Jesus, appears in Ignatius's vision at La Storta — his identification with Jesus carrying his cross — and in many of the key contemplations of the Spiritual Exercises. This mysticism stands alongside, not in competition with, other paths along the mystical way. At the same time, it broadens the notions of "mystic" and "mysticism," providing an alternative to spiritualities that are predominantly interior and otherworldly. Rather than moving away from history into the realm of the timeless, rather than turning one's back on human society and journeying into the inner expanses of one's own soul, the historical mystic turns toward God revealed *in* history and society.

Here, then, we see the essential elements of Pedro Arrupe's mysticism of open eyes. Metz coins this image to speak of the following of Jesus and the spirituality of the beatitudes. It corresponds closely to the biblical category of "poverty of spirit." Indeed, it seems to evoke the mysticism of Jesus himself as the synoptic Gospels portray him. Metz writes:

---

15. Ewert Cousins, "Franciscan Roots of Ignatian Meditation," in *Ignatian Spirituality in a Secular Age*, ed. George Schner, S.J. (Waterloo, Ont.: Wilfrid Laurier University, 1984), 60.

In the end Jesus did not teach an ascending mysticism of closed eyes, but rather a God-mysticism with an increased readiness for perceiving, a mysticism of open eyes, which sees more and not less. It is a mysticism that especially makes visible all invisible and inconvenient suffering, and — convenient or not — pays attention to it and takes responsibility for it, for the sake of a God who is a friend to human beings.[16]

It is a mysticism that *makes visible all invisible and inconvenient suffering,* a mysticism that *pays attention* and *takes responsibility,* engaging this broken world in order to find there its God. It is a mysticism of dangerous memory — Auschwitz for Metz, Hiroshima for Arrupe, the *memoria passionis, mortis et resurrectionis Jesu Christi* for all Christians — in which the mystical and the political are radically engaged and correlated.[17] Arrupe shows us that historical reality itself opens our eyes to the One who transcends that reality. He acknowledges that it was reality that opened his eyes. For example, while celebrating mass early on the first morning after the atomic bomb destroyed Hiroshima, he turned to face a mangled, bleeding, uncomprehending congregation of survivors: "I saw before my eyes many wounded, suffering terribly" (see below, p. 46). Some years later, after celebrating mass amid the appalling poverty of a Latin American slum, a "big fellow, whose fearful looks could have inspired fear," invited Arrupe to his home in order to express his thanks by sharing with the Jesuit General the only thing he had: a great view of the setting sun. *"Señor, see how*

16. Metz, *Passion for God,* 163.
17. For Metz's notion of "dangerous memory," in particular his understanding of the passion, death, and resurrection of Jesus as a dangerous memory, and his understanding of the mystical-political structure of Christian faith, see *Faith in History and Society* (New York: Seabury, 1980); "The Future in the Memory of Suffering," in J. B. Metz and J. Moltmann, *Faith and the Future* (Maryknoll, N.Y.: Orbis, 1995), 3–16.

beautiful it is!" (see p. 59). In both instances Arrupe saw reality and he saw through reality. He saw both the suffering and the beauty. He saw the tragic depths of our mortal poverty and the transcendent depths of our immortal destiny. He lived and prayed with opened and open eyes. This is his gift to us.

•

There are numerous ways to approach Pedro Arrupe, many doors into the rich corpus of his spiritual writings. The one chosen here can be summed up with the image of "looking over another's shoulders" in order to see what he sees. We look, as it were, over Arrupe's shoulders and attempt to read what he was reading, to assess events as he experienced them, and to glimpse the signs of the times that he was beholding and in the way he was beholding them. Accordingly, I have taken excerpts of Arrupe's writings (and, in a few instances, entire pieces) and organized them around four "fields of view" to which he attended: (1) his own journey of faith, (2) the faith, prayer, discipline, and devotion of the church in a time of renewal, (3) the life-story and Spiritual Exercises of St. Ignatius, and (4) the world of late modernity and an emerging postmodernity, above all, the world of the poor.

In chapter 1, we see Arrupe reading his own experience. He carefully describes his efforts to treat the survivors of the first atomic bomb. He shares some of his most poignant experiences of the Eucharist. The chapter ends with his thoughts as an older man looking back on fifty years of Jesuit life, a reflection on the very paradox of self-reflection, and a brief personal prayer that forms part of his "Invocation to the Trinity" (see below, p. 148). In chapter 2, Arrupe reflects on the life of Christian discipleship. This chapter begins with his personal love for Jesus Christ and reflects his devotion to the Sacred Heart of Jesus. It also addresses several of the most radical and demanding aspects of Christian discipleship: poverty, obedience, discernment, and mission. Chapter 2 ends with one of Arrupe's great prayers, his "prayer to Christ our Model." In chapter 3 Arrupe retells the story of Ignatius. He reflects on the logic and relevance of the Spiritual Exercises of Ignatius for our day and demonstrates that the mysticism of Ignatius is a mysticism of love. This chapter ends with another of Arrupe's great prayers, the "Invocation of the Trinity" with which he concludes his brilliant theological reflection on the trinitarian logic of Ignatian spirituality. Chapter 4 turns outward and gazes at the world as Arrupe beheld it during his years as General of the Society of Jesus. Here the angle is especially wide, taking in the social-political realities of world hunger, racism, poverty, martyrdom, and the overwhelming crisis of refugees, a sign of the times at once acute and chronic. This chapter includes two major pieces, his famous call for "Men and Women for Others," and his impassioned reflection on our world twenty-five years after Hiroshima. Chapter 4 ends with another great prayer of Arrupe, his "Invocation of the Holy Spirit." The brief Epilogue contains his final words as General and his final public homily.

Several other editorial notes are in order. My aim in this collection is to present an "Arrupe reader," to make Dom Pedro as accessible as possible, both in the way the selections are edited and in the decision to emend translations in several areas. I remove all but a very few footnotes, and cite quotations from scripture and the early Jesuits in the text. I drop most biblical citations not involving a direct quotation, along with many citations to the *Spiritual Exercises,* the letters of Ignatius, the official history of the Society of Jesus, and the like. While I utilize already existing English translations of Arrupe's works, I emend these translations in several ways by modernizing archaic English phrases, changing British spellings to American English, and

substituting English translations for most of the Latin phrases
Arrupe liked to sprinkle in his texts. In accordance with current usages, I routinely emend gender exclusive language and
racial designations that are no longer current, for example, substituting "human person" for "man" and "black people" for
"Negroes."

•

I wish to offer a few words of thanks. Conversations with many
people at the beginning of this project helped me envision the
final product. I wish to mention in particular Bill Sheahan, S.J.,
Margie Pfeil, Eileen Burke-Sullivan, Roger Haight, S.J., John
Dear, S.J., and James Martin, S.J., who originally suggested including Pedro Arrupe in the Modern Spiritual Masters series.
Along the way, conversations with John Padberg, S.J., Dave
Fleming, S.J., and Vinny O'Keefe, S.J., were invaluable. In addition, my research assistant, Robert Hamilton, saved me many
hours of work patiently preparing various manuscripts for edit-
ing. Kevin O'Brien, S.J., and James Sears, S.J., read earlier drafts
of this text, and their comments enabled me to shape it with
younger readers in mind. Many other colleagues and students
at Weston Jesuit School of Theology, and other friends in the
theological community, kept me on track throughout the process of preparing this text. Matt Ashley and Tom Massaro,
S.J., in particular, provided timely advice, the former with the
overall structure of the book and the latter with its numerous
details. Special thanks go to Robert Ellsberg, the editor-in-chief
of Orbis Books and editor of the Modern Spiritual Masters
series. Robert invited me to undertake this project, patiently
supported me throughout it, and offered excellent suggestions
for fine-tuning the final text. He is a perceptive reader and a
great editor.

Finally, I want to express my thanks to Father Pedro Arrupe, S.J. He was the Superior General of the Society of Jesus when I entered the order in 1976, and in many ways — ways too numerous to count — he inspired, taught, encouraged, and formed me as a Jesuit. He was a hero to those entrusted with my early formation in the Jesuits, and he quickly became my hero. More importantly, although I never met him personally, I count him among my spiritual friends and fathers in faith. Thank you, Pedro, for helping me learn how to learn and to see how to see.

1

His Own Life

I have the impression that my life is written in a single
sentence: "It has unfolded according to the will of God."
— *Pedro Arrupe*

SURVIVING THE ATOMIC BOMB

*On the Feast of the Transfiguration, August 6, 1945, the first
atomic bomb exploded over Hiroshima. Pedro Arrupe saw the
blinding flash of light. Moments later he heard its roar and felt
its seismic power throw him across the room and to the floor,
showering him in bits of broken glass and falling plaster. He
was thirty-seven, the master of novices and superior of a community of thirty-five men located in the town of Nagatsuka on
the outskirts of Hiroshima. In 1950 Arrupe traveled around the
world and spoke about his recollections of that experience. This
selection, which dates from that year, was first published as part
of a longer memoir in 1965. The companion piece located at the
end of chapter 4 was written in 1970, twenty-five years after the
atomic bomb destroyed Hiroshima.*

On the morning of August 6 something happened to break
the monotony of the previous months. At about 7:55 in the
morning a B-29 appeared. The air-raid alarm did not cause
us any undue worry since we had grown accustomed to seeing squadrons of a hundred planes flying over our heads. There
seemed to be no reason to be concerned. Ten minutes after the
alarm began to sound we were sure the enemy had left the city.
We then resumed our usual activities in peace.

I was in my room with another priest at 8:15 when suddenly
we saw a blinding light, like a flash of magnesium. Naturally we
were surprised and jumped up to see what was happening. As
I opened the door which faced the city, we heard a formidable
explosion similar to the blast of a hurricane. At the same time
doors, windows, and walls fell upon us in smithereens.

We threw ourselves or were thrown to the floor. I say we
were thrown because a German priest, who weighed over two
hundred pounds and had been resting against the window sill
of his room, found himself sitting in the hall several yards away
with a book in his hand. The shower of roof tiles, bricks, and
glass rained upon us. Three or four seconds seemed an eternity
because when one fears that a beam is about to crash down and
flatten one's skull, time is incredibly prolonged.

When we were able to stand, we went running through the
house. I had the responsibility for thirty-five young men who
were under my direction. I found none of them had even a
scratch. We went out into the garden to see where the bomb
had fallen since none of us doubted that that is what had happened. But when we got there, we looked at one another in
surprise: there was no hole in the ground, nor any sign of an
explosion. The trees and flowers all seemed quite normal. We
searched the rice fields surrounding our house, looking for the
site of the blast, but to no avail. After about fifteen minutes, we

noticed that in the direction of the city dense smoke arose. Soon we could see enormous flames.

We climbed a hill to get a better view. From there we could see a ruined city: before us was a decimated Hiroshima.

Since the houses were made of wood, paper, and straw, and it was at a time when the first meal of the day was being prepared in all the kitchens, the flames contacting the electric current turned the entire city into one enormous lake of fire within two and one half hours. . . .

I shall never forget my first sight of what was the result of the atomic bomb: a group of young women, eighteen or twenty years old, clinging to one another as they dragged themselves along the road. One had a blister that almost covered her chest; she had burns across half of her face, and a cut in her scalp caused probably by a falling tile, while great quantities of blood coursed freely down her face. On and on they came, a steady procession numbering some 150,000. This gives some idea of the scene of horror that was Hiroshima.

We continued looking for some way of entering the city, but it was impossible. We did the only thing that could be done in the presence of such mass slaughter: we fell on our knees and prayed for guidance, as we were destitute of all human help.

I had studied medicine many years earlier, and I ran back to the house to find medical supplies. I found the medicine chest under some ruins with the door off its hinges. I retrieved some iodine, aspirins, and bicarbonate of soda. Those were the only supplies at a time when 200,000 victims needed help. What could I do? Where to begin? Again I fell on my knees and implored God's help.

It was then that he helped me in a very special way, not with medications but with a simple and essential idea. We quickly decided to clean the house as best we could and tried to accommodate as many of the sick and wounded as we could possibly fit inside. We were able to take only 150.

The first thing that had to be done was to gather up extra food to provide those patients with sufficient energy to react against hemorrhages, fever, and infection caused by burns. Our young people, on foot or on bicycles, rushed about the outskirts of Hiroshima. Without thinking how or from where, they came dashing back with more fish, meat, eggs, and butter than we had seen in four years. With these we were able to care for our patients.

Some success crowned our efforts because, almost without realizing it, we were attacking from the outset the anemia and leukemia that would develop in the majority of the wounded who had been exposed to atomic radiation. We can rejoice that none of those hospitalized in our house died, except one child who suffered an attack of meningitis as a result of the accumulation of fluid on the brain and died the following day. All the rest survived.

While the young people were busy gathering food, I was trying to prepare the patients in a more scientific manner to react favorably. First of all, it was necessary to clean the three kinds of wounds we saw:

1. There were contusions caused by the collapse of buildings. These included fractures and cuts produced by jagged pieces of tile from falling roofs. Dirt and sawdust were encrusted in torn muscles and wounds. Those raw wounds had to be cleansed without anesthetic as we had neither chloroform nor ether nor morphine to assuage the terrible pain.

2. Other wounds were produced by fragments of wood or glass imbedded in the body without tearing the muscles.

3. The third group included all kinds of burns, some very serious. When asked how they were burned, the answer was often the same: they had been trapped under a collapsed smoldering building and as they tried to extricate themselves from under it, they were burned in the process. But there was another kind of burn whose cause no one could explain.

I asked one victim: "How were you burnt?"
I recall his answer, "I wasn't burnt, Father."
"Then, what happened to you?"
"I don't know. I saw a flash of light followed by a terrible explosion but nothing happened to me. Then, in a half hour I saw small, superficial blisters forming on my skin, and in four to five hours, there were large burnt areas on the skin which soon became infected. But there was no fire."

It was disconcerting. Today we know that it was the effects of infrared radiation which attacks the tissues and produces not only the destruction of the epidermis and the endodermis, but also of muscular tissue. The infections that followed resulted in the death of many and confused those treating the victims.

To cleanse the wounds it was necessary to puncture and open the blisters. We had in the house 150 people of whom one-third or one-half had open wounds. The work was painful because when one pierced a small blister, a tiny drop of water spilled out; but when one had to lance a blister that extended over half of a person's body, the discharge measured 150 cc [over half a cup]. At first we used nickel-plated pails, but after the third patient, seeing all there was ahead of us, we began to use all the kettles and basins we could find in the house.

The suffering was frightful, the pain excruciating, and it made bodies writhe like snakes, yet there was not a word of complaint. They all suffered in silence. In this respect the

Japanese manifest a certain superiority over occidentals: their self-control and stoicism are all the more admirable in the face of overwhelming provocation.

After twelve hours we were able to enter the city. As usually happens after great fires, an enormous amount of water vapor condenses and descends in torrential showers. In this way, at least, the burning embers were extinguished.

It was five in the afternoon. An indescribable spectacle met our gaze: a macabre vision which staggered the imagination. Before us lay a city completely destroyed. Through its streets we walked, stepping on ruins under which embers still felt warm. Any carelessness on our part could be fatal.

Much more terrible, however, was the tragic sight of those thousands of injured people begging for help. One such was a child who had a piece of glass imbedded in the pupil of his left eye, and another who had a large wooden splinter protruding like a dagger from between his ribs. Sobbing, he called out: "Father, save me!" Another victim was caught between two beams with his legs calcified up to the knees.

Moving along, we saw a young man running toward us half-crazed and calling for help. For twenty minutes he had been hearing his mother's voice as she lay buried under the rubble of what had been their home. The flames were already enveloping her body, and his efforts to lift the large wooden beams that held her captive had been in vain.

More heartbreaking, perhaps, were the cries of the children calling to their parents. Some two hundred children had perished in one school when the roof had collapsed on them.

At about ten o'clock in the evening we were able, at last, to locate the residence of our Fathers. All five were injured. Father Schiffer was in critical condition. He had suffered a head wound, which — in an effort to stop the bleeding and having nothing better at hand — they had wrapped in newspapers and a shirt somewhat like a turban. But they had overlooked another wound in the outer ear: a piece of glass had penetrated a small artery and he was slowly bleeding to death.

Using some wooden and bamboo planks, we improvised a stretcher on which we might carry him to Nagatsuka. Groaning in pain, but still smiling in true Japanese fashion, he said to me: "Father Arrupe, would you look at my back? I think there's something there." We turned him face down and, by the light of the torch, saw that his back was completely covered with wounds made by small pieces of glass.

With a razor blade I removed more than fifty fragments. After his operation, we moved slowly across the city, in the dark, toward our novitiate. Every hundred yards we had to stop so that both we and he might rest. During one of these pauses, we heard painful cries like those of someone near death. We could not find their source but someone, listening carefully, said: "It's underneath here somewhere." Sure enough, we had stepped on the ruins of a roof. Pushing some tiles to one side, we found an old lady half of whose body was burnt. She had been buried there all day and had barely a spark of life left. We removed her from under the rubble just as she was breathing her last.

We were to witness more horrible scenes that night. As we approached the river, the spectacle was awful beyond words. Fleeing the flames and availing themselves of low tide, the people lay across both shores, but in the middle of the night the tide began to rise, and the wounded, exhausted now and half buried in mud, could not move. The cries of those drowning are something I shall never forget.

At five in the morning, we finally arrived at our destination and began our first treatments on the Fathers. In spite of the urgency of our work, we had first stopped to celebrate our masses. Assuredly, it was in such moments of tragedy that we felt God most near to us. It is at such moments one feels in need of supernatural assistance.

The external surroundings in which the Holy Sacrifice was being offered were not such as might promote sensible devotion. In turning around to say "Dominus Vobiscum," I saw before my eyes many wounded, suffering terribly. While reading the Epistle and the Gospel, I had to be careful not to touch with my feet the children that lay so close to me. They wanted to see closely this stranger who was wearing such odd clothing and performing those ceremonies they had never seen before. In spite of it all, I do not think I have ever said mass with such devotion.

After mass, when we began to think what more we could do, since natural healing with the help of a good diet was not enough, the Lord came to our aid once again.

At eight in the morning, one of our employees came to me with a sack in his hand, and said: "Father, I wanted to help these poor people, too, and, looking here and there to see what I might find, I came upon this sack filled with little bottles that look like medicine. See if they are any good."

The contents were over thirty pounds of boric acid. There lay the solution to our problem. Using our underwear and sheets we made many bandages and began our work which, though primitive, gave us fine results.

We would place bandages on the wounds, keeping them moist all day with an antiseptic solution of boric acid. In this way, the pain was somewhat relieved and the lesion was kept relatively clean and in contact with the air. The discharge from the wounds would adhere to the dressing, and by changing it four or five times a day we were able to assure asepsis. Continuing this curative process, we could see, in less than a week, the gradual formation of granulations of scar tissue which brought, slowly but surely, a total cure to all. We had no cases of malignant degeneration of the scars....

Much could be written of individual cases that we encountered in that holocaust. We shall briefly describe a few.

I was in Nagatsuka treating some wounded when a young couple came to me. The woman was very well since she had been out of the city at the moment of the explosion. Her husband, a young man of twenty-two, was in a lamentable state. He could hardly move. Assisted by his wife who was dragging him along, he came into the house. A trail of pus followed his entrance. Half of his body was one big wound.

It was the most serious case I had yet seen, and I thought to myself that the poor man had come to die in our midst. But he, when he realized I was hesitating, took hold of my hand and said in anguish:

"Father, help me!"

And his wife, taking my other hand, explained:

"Father, we're married just one month. Save my husband!"

I didn't know what to say. At a moment like that a thousand thoughts pass through one's mind all at once. Finally, I answered, almost meditatively: "Very well, let's see what we can do, but it's going to hurt a lot."

Fixing his eyes on me, he said: "Hurt me all you want, I can bear it."

Accordingly, we put him on the operating table, which was my office desk, and began to clean the wounds. The poor man, how he twisted and turned! It had to be done in cold blood because the pus had hardened underneath the burns, yet, in the midst of his pain, he kept repeating: "Father, don't hesitate to hurt me; I can take it, but just save me."

Someone whispered in my ear: "Would it be possible to cause him less anguish?"

But this was impossible. I had to become like an executioner
to this man if I was to save his life. And this I was for two and
a half hours. At the end he was prostrate with suffering and I,
exhausted with the tension I felt while crucifying him with so
much pain.

In Japan, since the walls are so thin, one can hear every word
spoken on the other side; but the young man, forgetting this,
as soon as we were out of sight, let go with a volley of verbal
abuse against his poor wife using every epithet in the dictionary,
thus venting the accumulated anger caused by those hours of
torment.

She remained passive. As a good Japanese woman, she listened to him smilingly, lighting his cigarette, wiping away
perspiration, and giving him something cool to drink. And there
she remained by his side day and night. We could never find out
when she slept.

After eight months this couple left our house. On an April
morning, I saw them walking down the hill by the garden, smiling, happy, and baptized. I felt a deep joy at that moment which
fully compensated for all the pain of the past eight months. If
we had not treated that young man he most certainly would
have died.

Among all the cases we treated, perhaps those that caused
us the most suffering were the children. Everyone knows that
in Japan children are adored. They take extreme care with their
education to such a degree that there is no illiteracy in Japan: all
go to primary and secondary schools; all know how to read and
write. At the time of the atomic bomb most of the children were
in their respective schools. For that reason, during the explosion thousands of children were separated from their parents;
many were wounded and cast into the streets without being able
to fend for themselves. We brought all we could to Nagatsuka

and began treating them immediately so as to prevent infection and fever.

We had absolutely no anesthetics, and some of the children were horribly wounded. One had a cut from ear to ear as a result of a beam that fell on his head. The edge of the wound was over half an inch wide; the injured region of the scalp was filled with clay and pieces of glass. The screams of the poor child during his treatment so upset the entire house that we had no choice but to tie him into a cart with sheets and take him to the top of a hillock near the house. That spot was converted into an amphitheater where we could work, and the child could scream all he wanted without making everyone else a nervous wreck.

Our hearts were torn apart during these treatments, but greater was the consolation at being able to restore the children to their parents. Through the Japanese police, who were well organized, we were able to contact all the families whose children we had in the house. Memorable are those scenes of reunion with children that were thought dead in the explosion, and now were found alive and well, or at least in the process of healing. Those mothers and fathers, overcome with joy, did not know how to express their gratitude, and throwing themselves at our feet, reminded us of the Acts of the Apostles when pagans, falling on their knees, adored the disciples of Christ as gods.

Apart from all these understandable events, there was one that disconcerted us greatly. Many who were in the city at the moment of the explosion and had suffered no apparent injuries whatsoever, but who, nevertheless, after a few days felt weak and came to us saying they felt a terrible interior heat, that perhaps they had inhaled a poisonous gas, and in a short time they were dead.

The first case occurred for me when I was treating an elderly man for two deep wounds on his back. A man came to me and said: "Please, Father, come to my house because my son tells me he has a very bad sore throat."

Since the man I was treating was gravely ill, I answered: "It's probably a cold. Give him some aspirin and make him perspire; you'll see he'll get well." Within two hours the boy died.

Later a girl of thirteen came weeping and said: "Father, look what's happening to me."

And opening her mouth, she showed me bleeding gums, small sores on the lining of the mouth and an acute pharyngitis. She showed me too how her hair was falling out in her hands in bunches. In two days she was dead....

Of the dead, fifty thousand died the moment of the explosion itself, another two hundred thousand during the following weeks, and others much later as a result of wounds or radiation. Until the day after the explosion, we did not know that we were dealing with the first atomic bomb to explode in our world.

At first, without electricity or radio, we were cut off from the rest of the world. The following day cars and trains began arriving from Tokyo and Osaka with help for Hiroshima. They stayed in the outskirts of the city, and when we questioned them as to what had happened, they answered very mysteriously: "The first atomic bomb has exploded."

"But what is the atomic bomb?"

They would answer: "The atom bomb is a terrible thing."

"We have seen how terrible it is; but what is it?"

And they would repeat: "It's the atomic bomb...the atomic bomb."

They knew nothing but the name. It was a new word that was coming for the first time into the vocabulary. Besides, the knowledge that it was the atomic bomb that had exploded was no help to us at all from a medical standpoint, as no one in the world knew its full effects on the human organism. We were, in effect, the first guinea pigs in such experimentation.

But from a missionary standpoint, they did challenge us when they said: "Do not enter the city because there is a gas in the air that kills for seventy years." It is at such times that one feels most a priest, when one knows that in the city there are 50,000 bodies which, unless they are cremated, will cause a terrible plague. There were besides some 120,000 wounded to care for. In light of these facts, a priest cannot remain outside the city just to preserve his life. Of course, when one is told that in the city there is a gas that kills, one must be very determined to ignore that fact and go in. And we did. And we soon began to raise pyramids of bodies and pour fuel on them to set them afire.   — "Surviving the Atomic Bomb" in *RR* 22–39

RECOGNIZING THE "HAND OF THE LORD" AT EUCHARIST

One cannot comment on the faith of Father Arrupe without reference to the Eucharist. It was the center of his life of prayer, which he called "the most important act of the entire daily routine." Arrupe frequently wrote about the importance of the Eucharist for St. Ignatius, for the work of the Society of Jesus, and for the ongoing life and mission of the church. In the selections that follow, he speaks about the importance of the Eucharist in his own life and the implications of a genuine eucharistic faith and piety for all Christians today. The first four selections presented here are taken from his talk to the Youth Eucharistic Movement, a gathering of some fourteen hundred high school boys, which met in Assisi on September 6, 1979. The fifth, **Eucharist and Hunger,** *is the opening section of his address to the Worldwide Eucharistic Congress that met in Philadelphia, Pennsylvania, in 1976. The sixth selection,* **The**

Mass in "My Cathedral," comes from a personal memoir first published in his collection of writings on the Sacred Heart, Him Alone*).*

Miracle at Lourdes

I shall relate some of my own experiences which were connected with the Eucharist and in which I recognize the hand of the Lord who led me and still leads me in my way of life. But I am sure that you also can reflect on your own experience up till now and on the way in which the Lord is guiding you on the path of your life.

The first of my Eucharist experiences was closely connected with my vocation as a Jesuit.... The experience was that of a miracle which I saw at Lourdes during the procession of the Blessed Sacrament on the esplanade that lies in front of the basilica. Some weeks after the death of my father I had gone to Lourdes with my family, since we wished to spend the summer in quiet, peaceful, and spiritual surroundings. It was the middle of August. I stayed at Lourdes for a whole month. And since I was a medical student, I was able to obtain a special permission to study closely the sick who came seeking a cure.

One day I was in the esplanade with my sisters a little before the procession of the Blessed Sacrament. A cart pushed by a woman of middle age passed in front of us. One of my sisters exclaimed: "Look at that poor boy in the cart." It was a young man of around twenty, all twisted and contorted by polio. His mother was reciting the rosary in a loud voice and from time to time she would say with a sigh: "María Santísima, help us." It was a truly moving sight, and I remembered the plea which the sick turned toward Jesus: "Lord, cleanse me from this leprosy!" She hastened to take her place in the row which the bishop was to pass carrying the Blessed Sacrament in a monstrance.

The moment came when the bishop was to bless the young man with the host. He looked at the monstrance with the same faith with which the paralytic mentioned in the Gospel must have looked at Jesus. After the bishop had made the sign of the cross with the Blessed Sacrament, the young man rose cured from the cart, as the crowd filled with joy cried out: "Miracle! Miracle!"

Thanks to the special permission which I had, I was later able to assist at the medical examinations. The Lord had truly cured him. There is no need to tell you of what I felt and my state of mind at that moment. I had come from the School of Medicine in Madrid, where I had had so many professors (some truly renowned) and so many companions who had no faith and who always ridiculed miracles. But I had been an eyewitness of a true miracle worked by Jesus Christ in the Eucharist, by that same Jesus Christ who had during the course of his life cured so many who were ill and paralytic. I was filled with an immense joy. I seemed to be standing by the side of Jesus. And as I sensed his almighty power, the world that stood around me began to appear extremely small. I returned to Madrid. My books fell from my hands. The lessons, the experiments which had so thrilled me before now seemed so very empty. My comrades asked me: "What's happening to you this year? You are like one who has been stunned!" Yes, I was like one stunned by that impression which every day grew more disconcerting. The one thing that remained fixed in my mind and in my heart was the image of the host as it was raised in benediction and of the paralyzed boy who had leapt from his cart. Three months later I entered the novitiate of the Society of Jesus in Loyola, Spain.

— "Eucharist and Youth" in *OA* 289–90

Mass on Mount Fujiyama

Every mass is a mass for the world and in the world. I remember the mass which I celebrated at the top of the famous Mount Fujiyama, at a height of more than eleven thousand feet. I had climbed it with one of my religious brothers. At that time the climb was made almost entirely on foot. One could go on horseback only to a height of about thirty-three hundred feet. It was necessary to reach the summit by four in the morning to be able to see the marvelous panorama since by six the peak was covered with clouds and could no longer be seen.

We arrived on time and celebrated mass in the most complete solitude. It was shortly after I arrived in Japan. I was living through the first impressions of a new environment, and my mind was bubbling with a great number of projects for the conversion of the whole of Japan. We had climbed Fujiyama so that we might be able to offer to the Eternal Father the Sacrifice of the Immaculate Lamb for the salvation of all Japan at the highest point in all that country. The climb had been most tiring since we had to hasten in order to arrive on time. Several times we thought of Abraham and Isaac as they climbed a mountain to offer their sacrifice. Once we had reached the top, the sight of the rising sun was stupendous. It raised our spirits and disposed them for the celebration of the Holy Sacrifice. Till then I had never celebrated mass in such conditions. Above us the blue sky expanded like the cupola on an immense temple — brilliant and majestic. Before us were all the people of Japan, at that time some eighty million who did not know God. My mind ranged out beyond the lofty vaulting of the sky to the throne of the divine majesty, the seat of the Blessed Trinity. I seemed to see the holy city of the heavenly Jerusalem. I seemed to see Jesus Christ and with him St. Francis Xavier, the first apostle of Japan, whose hair had become white in the course of a few months because of the sufferings he had to endure. I also was being confronted by that same Japan as Xavier had been. The future was entirely unknown. If I had then known how much I would have to suffer, my hands would have trembled as I raised the sacred host. On that summit so near to heaven it seemed to me that I understood better the mission which God had entrusted to me. I descended from it with a renewed enthusiasm. That Eucharist had made me feel the grandeur of the everlasting God and universal Lord. At the same time I had felt that I was an "assistant," a sharer in the labor of Jesus Christ in the great redemptive mission entrusted to him by his Father. I could repeat with more sincerity and conviction the words of Isaiah — "Here I am, send me" (Isa. 6:8) — or those of St. Francis Xavier — "I am! Behold me."

— "Eucharist and Youth" in *OA* 292–93

Eucharist and Solitary Confinement

Another type of eucharistic experience is that which shows us the value that the most Blessed Sacrament has for us when we have been in intimate and prolonged contact with him during our life and we sense the lack of this sacrament when we are not able to receive it. At such a time we appreciate the great role which Jesus, our friend, companion, and consoler, has in our life if we have been and are habitually nourished by the Eucharist. . . .

I myself personally experienced this deep sense of pain for the lack of the Eucharist during the thirty-three days that I was imprisoned in Japan, but there was also at the same time a feeling of the faithful and consoling presence of Our Lord. The enemies of Christianity had made a thousand accusations against me. They were angry, since they saw that while they were trying to put obstacles in the way to conversions, a good number of young people were turning to the church and were receiving baptism. The war broke out in Japan on the feast of the Immaculate Conception, 1941, with the attack of Pearl Harbor. The military police immediately put me in jail, in a cell with an area of four square meters. I did not know why they had put me there, and I was not told why for a long time, and only at the end of my confinement.

I passed the days and nights in the cold of December entirely alone and without a bed, or table, or anything else but a mat on which to sleep. I was tormented by my uncertainty on why I had been imprisoned. This provoked a kind of self-torture because of the presumptions, suspicions, and fears that I had done something that could have been a source of harm to others. But I was above all tortured by not being able to say mass, at not being able to receive the Eucharist. What loneliness there was! I then appreciated what the Eucharist means to a priest, to a Jesuit, for whom the mass and the tabernacle are the very center of his life. I saw myself dirty, unshaven, famished, and chilled to the bone without being able to talk with anyone. But I felt even more anguish for my Christians who were perhaps suffering because of me. And above all there was no mass. How much I learned then! I believe that it was the month in which I learned the most in all my life. Alone as I was, I learned the knowledge of silence, of loneliness, of harsh and severe poverty, the interior conversation with "the guest of the soul" who had never shown himself to be more "sweet" than then.

During those hours, those days, those weeks of silence and reflection I understood in a more illuminating and consoling way the words of Christ: "Remember what I have told you: a servant is not more important than his master. If they have persecuted me, they will also persecute you" (John 15:20).

I was interrogated for thirty-six hours in a row. I was asked matters that were very touchy to answer, and I was myself astonished by the "wisdom" and the fitness of my replies. It was a proof of the saying of the Gospel: "Do not be concerned about what you must say to defend yourselves. I shall give you the right words and I shall give you such wisdom that all your adversaries will not be able to resist and much less defeat you" (Luke 21:14–15).

When my sufferings were becoming more cruel, I experienced a moment of great consolation. It was Christmas night. My mind went back to so many happy Christmases, to the three masses which I was able to celebrate that night. What remembrances filled my mind! But none of all this was now possible. I was alone, without mass. Instead of Christmas it seemed more like Good Friday! Just then when my Christmas was being changed into the passion and that blessed night into a sad Gethsemane, I heard a strange sound near one of the windows. It was the soft murmur of many voices which, with muted accents, sought to escape detection. I began to listen. If any of you have been in prison waiting for a sentence, you would appreciate the anxiety with which I followed those sounds which were now of themselves becoming an immediate source of suspicion. Such are the fears that one feels within the four walls where one is detained.

Suddenly, above the murmur that was reaching me, there arose a soft, sweet, consoling Christmas carol, one of the songs which I had myself taught to my Christians. I was unable to contain myself. I burst into tears. They were my Christians who, heedless of the danger of being themselves imprisoned, had come to console me, to console their *Shimpu Sarna* (their priest), who was away that Christmas night which hitherto we had always celebrated with such great joy. What a contrast between that thoughtfulness and the injustice of senseless imprisonment!

The song with those accents and inflections which are not taught or learned poured forth from a touching kindness and

sincere affection. It lasted for a few minutes; then there was silence again. They had gone and I was left to myself. But our
spirits remained united at the altar on which soon after would
descend Jesus. I felt that he also descended into my heart, and
that night I made the best spiritual communion of all my life.

— "Eucharist and Youth" in *OA* 296–300

In the Midst of the Poor

A few years ago I was visiting a Jesuit province in Latin America. I was invited, with some timidity, to celebrate a mass in a
suburban slum, in a *favela,* the poorest in the region as they
told me. There were around a hundred thousand people living
there in the midst of mud since the town had been built along
the side of a depression and became almost completely flooded
whenever it rained. I readily accepted since I know from experience that visits to the poor are most instructive: they do much
good for the poor, but one also learns much from them.

The mass was held in a small structure all patched together
and open. Since there was no door, cats and dogs came and
went without any problem. The mass began. The songs were
accompanied by a guitar which was strummed by one who was
not exactly an expert, but the results seemed marvelous to me.
The words were as follows: "To love is to give oneself, to forget
oneself, by seeking that which can make another happy." And
they continued: "How beautiful it is to live for love, how great
it is to have to give. To give joy and happiness, to give oneself,
this is love." "If you love as you love yourself, and give yourself for others, you will see that there is no egoism which you
cannot conquer. How beautiful it is to live for love."

Gradually as the song went on, I felt a knot in my throat, and
I had to force myself to continue with the mass. Those people,

who seemed to have nothing, were ready to give themselves to share their joy and happiness.

When we arrived at the consecration and I raised the host in the midst of an absolute silence, I perceived the joy of the Lord who remains with his beloved. As Jesus says: "He has sent me to bring the good news to the poor" (Luke 4:18), "Blessed are the poor in spirit" (Matt. 5:3).

Soon after, when I was distributing communion and was looking at their faces, dry, hard, and tanned by the sun, I noticed that large tears like pearls were running down many of them. They were meeting Jesus, their only consolation. My hands trembled.

At the end a big fellow, whose fearful looks could have inspired fear, told me: "Come to my house. I have something to honor you." I remained uncertain, not knowing whether I should accept or not, but the priest who was accompanying me said: "Go with him, Father; the people are very good." I went to his house, which was a half-falling shack. He made me sit down on a rickety chair. From where I was seated the sun could be seen as it was setting. The fellow said to me: "Señor, see how beautiful it is!" And we remained silent for some minutes. The sun disappeared. The man added: "I did not know how to thank you for all that you have done for us. I have nothing to give you, but I thought that you would like to see this sunset. It pleased you, didn't it? Good evening." He then gave me his hand. As I was leaving, I thought: "I have met very few hearts that are so kind." — "Eucharist and Youth" in *OA* 302–3

Eucharist and Hunger

"Lord, it is good for us to be here" (Mark 9:5). It is good to be with you and share with you this wonderful celebration. But suppose the hungry of the world were also here with us this morning. Let us think only of those who are going to die of starvation today, the day of our Symposium of Hunger. There would be thousands of them, probably more than all of us who are gathered in this hall. Let us try to see them: their bodies weak and emaciated, their outstretched hands, their weak and fading voices, their terrible silence: "Give us bread...give us bread for we are dying of hunger!"

And if, at the end of our discussions on "the Eucharist and the Hunger for Bread," as we left the hall, we had to pick our way through this mass of dying bodies, how could we claim that our Eucharist is the Bread of Life? How could we pretend to be announcing and sharing with others the same Lord who said: "I come that they may have life, and have it more abundantly" (John 10:10).

It matters little if these starving people are physically before our eyes here and now or scattered throughout the world: on the streets of Calcutta or in the rural areas of Sahel or Bangladesh. The tragedy and injustice of their death are the same wherever it takes place. And wherever it does take place, we who are here this morning have our share of responsibility. For, in the Eucharist, we receive Jesus Christ who will one day ask us: "I was hungry, did you give me to eat? I was thirsty, did you give me to drink? I tell you solemnly, insofar as you neglected to do this to one of the least of these, my brothers or sisters, you neglected to do it to me" (see Matt. 25:42, 45).

Yes, we are all responsible, all involved! In the Eucharist, Jesus becomes the voice of those who have no voice. He speaks for the powerless, the oppressed, the poor, the hungry. In fact, he takes their place. And if we close our ears to their cries, we are shutting out his voice too. If we refuse to help them, then our faith is indeed dead as St. James tells us so clearly: "If one of the brothers or one of the sisters is in need of clothes and has not enough food to live on and one of you says to them, 'I wish you well; keep yourself warm and eat plenty,' without giving them these bare necessities of life, then what good is that? Faith is like that: if good works do not go with it, it is quite dead" (James 2:15–17).

Brothers and sisters, let us be honest! Most of us here this morning are well fed and in reasonably comfortable circumstances. God grant we may not merit the condemnation St. James reserves for the selfish rich, whether individuals or nations, who refuse to give bread to the hungry or to raise up the poor! "Start crying, weep for the miseries that are coming to you.... On earth you have had a life of comfort and luxury; in the time of slaughter you went on eating to your heart's content. It was you who condemned the innocent and killed them; they offered you no resistance" (James 5:1, 5–6).

— "The Eucharist and Hunger" in *JF* 172–73

The Mass in "My Cathedral"

A mini-cathedral! Just eighteen feet by twelve. A little chapel which was prepared after the death of my predecessor, Father Janssens, for the new General, whoever this might be! Providence willed that this should be myself. I am grateful to the one who had the idea: he could not have interpreted the wish of this new General better. The planner of this tiny chapel may have desired to give the new General a quiet and convenient place to celebrate the mass in greater privacy and where he might visit the Blessed Sacrament without leaving his rooms. Possibly he did not think that the little oratory would be the fountain of incalculable power and dynamism for the whole Society, a place of inspiration, consolation, and strength — even a living room! It was going to be the room for relaxing in the most active leisure, where doing nothing everything is done! As the idle Mary drinking in the Master's words, much more active than her sister Martha! Where the Master's glance and mine cross each other, where one learns much in silence.

The General would have the Lord all the time, every day, next to him, with just a partition between them; the very Lord who was able to enter through the closed doors of the upper room, who made himself present among his disciples, the one who would be invisibly present in so many conversations and meetings in my office.

They call this little room the private chapel of the General. It is a teacher's chair and a sanctuary: Tabor and Gethsemane, Bethlehem and Golgotha, Manresa and La Storta! Ever the same, ever different. If its walls could speak! Four walls that enclose an altar, a tabernacle, a crucifix, a Marian icon, a *zabuton* (a Japanese cushion), a Japanese painting, one lamp. Nothing else is needed; that's all: a victim, a sacrificial altar, the standard of the cross, a Mother, a burning flame that is slowly being consumed while giving light and warmth, and love expressed by two Japanese characters: God–Love.

Here is a program of life: a life being consumed in love, crucified with Jesus, in Mary's company being offered to God, as the victim which is offered to the Father day after day on the altar. . . . This cathedral is the theater of the most important act of the entire daily routine: the mass. Christ is the true and supreme priest, the Word made flesh. It is a divine attribute to be contained in the smallest place and not to be circumscribed by the universe: this tabernacle or little tent is not too small for him, but the entire universe is not big enough to hold him.

Each mass has an infinite value but under some personal circumstances and in some special moments this quality of infinitude is felt more deeply. There is no doubt that the fact of being the General of the Society of Jesus with its twenty-seven thousand men consecrated to the Lord and totally dedicated to

collaborate with Jesus Christ the Savior, in all sorts of difficult apostolates, which may at times lead to sacrificing life in
a bloody martyrdom, carries with it a weight of responsibility
and a profound sense of universality of its own.

●

My position between God and the Society of Jesus, as a priest
and during the celebration of the Eucharist, is that of a "media-
tor between God and human beings" to govern the whole body
of the Society. As Ignatius writes in the *Constitutions,* "The superior will do this primarily by his prayer which is full of desires
and by his sacrifices, to obtain the grace of preservation and
development. On his own part he should hold these means in
high esteem and have great confidence in our Lord, since these
are the most efficacious means of gaining grace from his Divine
Majesty, the source of what is longed for." The office of General thus considered appears in all its depth and in clear light:
"morning after morning the Lord God opens my ear that I may
hear" (Isa. 50:4–5).

— "The Mass in 'My Cathedral'" in *HA* 46–48, 50

FIFTY YEARS AS A JESUIT

*On January 15, 1977, Arrupe celebrated his fiftieth jubilee as
a Jesuit. At the anniversary mass held in the Church of the
Gesù, in Rome, Arrupe preached the following homily. In this
personal reflection he reflects on three religious leaders who inspired him and three great passions at the center of his religious
vocation. The homily was previously published in English under
the title "Three Models and Three Loves."*

Today's celebration is only one of many you have attended on the occasion of anniversaries and jubilees. All have had one common denominator: on the one hand, a genuine sense and admission of smallness on the part of a man humbly conscious of his unfaithfulness, and on the other, an acknowledgment of the Lord's generosity and a deep feeling of gratitude toward him. This dialectic between a human person's smallness and limitations and the greatness of the Creator runs like a master thread through each personal history. All, from this point of view, are alike, but at the same time they each reveal ever differing aspects and developments. Each one differs from the other. Each one has his or her own distinctive character. Each one has his or her own particular history, one that does not repeat any other, and one that will be repeated by no other.

In listening to these personal histories one senses in each of them something that is unspoken because it cannot be uttered, a personal secret that not even the individuals themselves fully understand. This sphere that is hidden, or half-hidden, even from ourselves is the area that is truly interesting because it is most intimate, deepest, most personal. It is the area of closest relationship between God, who is love and who loves each one in a different way, and the human being who from the depths of his being gives a response that is unique because there is not nor will there ever be his like. It is the secret of wondrous trinitarian love, a love that intrudes when it wills into the life of each, in a manner that is unforeseen, inexpressible, irrational, irresistible, and yet one that is nonetheless wonderfully decisive. No individual's life, as a life, can be defined or expressed in "Aristotelian" categories. The reason is because there is at work in each life a double vital force, one human, the other divine, and the latter is God's love that surpasses all intelligence — "how impossible," as St. Paul says, "to penetrate his motives or understand his methods" (Rom. 11:33).

Reviewing the course of my seventy years, of which fifty have been in the Society, I cannot help but recognize that the decisive stages, the radical turning points in my life's path, have always been unexpected, I might even say irrational. But sooner or later, in every instance, I have had to recognize the hand of God that gave the helm a bold twist. My vocation to the Society of Jesus, after having begun the study of medicine, a subject that interested me so greatly, and right in the middle of my university career; my vocation to Japan (a mission for which I had no attraction at all prior to God's call), which my superiors refused me for ten years while they were preparing me to become one day a professor of moral theology; my presence in the city over which the first atom bomb exploded; my election as General of the Society...these were such sudden and unexpected happenings and at the same time they carried with them so clearly the "mark" of God, that in fact I have viewed and still view them as a series of those "irruptions" by which God's loving providence is pleased to reveal its presence and its absolute dominion over each of us. The reactions that I experienced made me think of the words of Isaiah: "What a wretched state I am in! I am lost, for I am a man of unclean lips" (Isa. 6:5); or of Jeremiah: "Ah, Lord God; look...I am a child!" (Jer. 1:6); or of Moses: "Who am I to go to Pharaoh?" (Exod. 3:11).

I have said that you are assisting at one of those many anniversaries in which the smallness of a man (and here today I am that man) evokes amazement and gratitude when God's blessings are recalled. Amazement and gratitude, not only, or not so much, over the privileged, decisive, or important moments of my life, but above all over the series of uninterrupted and immeasurable graces I have received each day during the course of everyday life in a monotonous, humdrum, and ordinary existence. All these memories make me wish that my life could have been, or at least might be from now on, an unending "Magnificat."

This indeed is the sentiment that sweeps over me when I experience a clear awareness and lively sense of my smallness, joined to a certain unshakable feeling of security in the various posts of responsibility that obedience had placed on my weak shoulders. The experience I have felt is that "I will always be with you" (Judg. 6:16), the guarantee that the Lord gives but that always leaves an uneasy doubt on one's part whether "the condition will be fulfilled" or whether he will remain faithful. These are the lights and shadows of human insecurity that cannot call in question the security that derives from God's help.

Abraham, Paul, Xavier

Reflecting above all on these more recent years, I have discovered three figures that symbolize my state of soul. In a way, they are patrons and models that help and instruct me.

1. The first is Abraham, the resolute and generous patriarch who responded promptly to God's call to go forth from his own land, to take up his abode elsewhere, in a place that was unknown to him. Abraham set out on his way, leaving behind his own land, the house of his father...in search of "the land I will show you," as the Lord had said to him (Gen. 12:1). This is a type of vocation that, especially in the circumstances of some years back, seemed to me to be filled with inspiration. A call from God, an unexpected "intrusion" by God, an uncharted assignment — "I will show you" — and a response that might seem to be unreasonable and whose fulfillment will involve one's whole life. Still, Abraham started out straightaway on the road, sustained by a blind trust: "Though

it seemed Abraham's hope could not be fulfilled, he hoped and he believed" (Rom. 4:18).

This was my inner state in the first years of my life in the Society, at the moment when I set out for Japan, and especially on the day I was elected General. This last experience was an exodus, much more radical, amid extreme uncertainty and under an enormous burden of responsibility; an exodus out of a whole world of habits, practices, ideas, choices, from which I had to take leave in order to face up to a whole set of others that were very imprecise and lacking clarity and definition; an exodus out of a world filled with securities fashioned along the centuries-old traditions of the church and of the Society, in order to set out on paths that would bring me into a world that was still "in the making," unknown, but to which God called us through the voices of the Council, the pope, and the General Congregations. These were paths filled with unknown elements and challenges, but also filled with hopes and opportunities; paths that were and continue to be God's paths.

The figure of Abraham has always been for me an inexhaustible source of inspiration. "Where is the Society heading?" people have asked me. My reply has always been: "Where God is leading it." In other words: "I don't know. But there is one thing I do know and it is that God is carrying us along somewhere. Let us go forward confidently. Let us go forward with the church that is guided by the Holy Spirit. I know that God is leading us toward a new land, the promised land, his land. He knows where it is. Our task is only to follow him."

This stance, which without faith is absolutely unreasonable and imprudent, with faith, with the trust of Abraham, becomes clear, secure, consoling. One who reasons according to God's logic recognizes it as the only truly reasonable, uniquely prudent position. This spirit of self-abandonment, of hurling oneself blindly into the arms of God, is a source of consolation and strength that can be experienced only through the mediation of faith.

2. Naturally, on such pathways there cannot fail to be difficulties, misunderstandings, obstacles. Human strength is not enough because what God asks of us is "beyond our capacities." But here I come up against my second model and patron, St. Paul. His advice is inspired and has never led me astray. "I hardly deserve the name apostle; but by God's grace that is what I am" (1 Cor. 15:10). "There is nothing I cannot master with the help of the One who gives me strength" (Phil. 4:13). "With God on our side who can be against us" (Rom. 8:31)? In our effort to follow the Lord, we beg continually, as did St. Paul, for the moment when "you will be told what you have to do" (Acts 9:6). And we hear his reply: "If you remain in me and my words remain in you, you may ask what you will and you shall get it" (John 15:7). The outcome is certain: God's omnipotence requires that it come about, "since no one can oppose his will" (Rom. 9:19).

But "how rich are the depths of God — how deep his wisdom and knowledge" (Rom. 11:33), and thus, the outcome does not consist precisely in the fact that everything works out to a happy ending, that everything turns out well. In God's way of thinking the cross holds a privileged place and leaves a distinguishing mark: for him who has faith, this "madness," this "obstacle" is the "wisdom of God" (1 Cor. 1:22–25). For this reason St. Paul, our model, writes: "As for me, the only thing I can boast about is the cross of our Lord Jesus Christ" (Gal. 6:14).

3. My third model and patron, this time from the Society of Jesus, is St. Francis Xavier. Xavier, the man whose real source of apostolic energy was trust in God: the more one trusts in himself and in his own resources, the less strength he will

have. Xavier, who understood brilliantly the value of the cross and of suffering, up to the very point where his prayer became one of "more, more" when it was a matter of the cross, and of "enough, Lord, enough," when he was the recipient of consolations.

These three figures of Abraham, Paul, and Xavier have been a continuing inspiration to me because they incarnate the spirit of God in a realistic interpretation of perfect indifference, the ideal of the third degree of Ignatian humility. They realize to perfection the meaning of a saying of Ignatius: "Trust in God as if the success of things depended wholly on you and not at all on God; but set to work as if God alone were to do everything and you do nothing."

The Society, the Church, Christ

During these fifty years of religious life with their varied experiences, certain particular loves have grown and increased in me almost unawares. They have, moreover, the proper characteristic of all true love: the more suffering, the more love.

1. The first is love of the Society of Jesus. A simple and filial love, from the time of the novitiate, and one that without losing any simplicity went on to acquire through life's experience an extraordinary depth and robustness.

The Society is understood as the expression and incarnation of the Ignatian charism. To the extent that the evangelical intuition of this charism is known intimately, the more its simplicity emerges. It is the intuition of love that succeeds in uniting elements that, without such love, would seem to be irreconcilable. Or at least they would give rise to dichotomies and tensions that restrain the true apostolic drive: action/contemplation, faith/justice, obedience/freedom, poverty/efficiency, unity/pluralism, a sense of the particular/a sense of the universal. St. Ignatius, on the contrary, discovers marvelous solutions that unite what seem to be in conflict and thus yield the greatest apostolic effectiveness.

The Society is made up of persons. This is one of the greatest spiritual experiences that a General can have: that of understanding spiritually, as it were "from within," so many members of the Society — to enter into contact with them in very varied ways and circumstances, directly and indirectly. For me this has been one of the greatest comforts and stimuli — to see the virtue and the quality of members of the Society. It is a little like what Xavier must have felt when he wrote from Amboino to his companions in Europe: "Because I never forget you....I want you to understand, dearest brethren, that I have torn from the letters you have sent me your own names, written in your own hands...and I carry these constantly with me for the sake of the consolation that I receive from them." Or when he wrote to the Jesuits in Goa: "If the hearts of those who love each other in Christ could be seen in this present life, believe me, brethren, you could see yourselves clearly in mine. And if, when you looked in it you did not recognize yourselves, that would be because I hold you in such high esteem, and on account of your virtue you hold yourselves in such low rank, that your humility renders you unable to see and recognize yourselves in it."

This is one of the greatest grounds I have for optimism when I think of the future of the Society. The same Lord who has given such vocations and so many accompanying graces to these sons of Ignatius, cannot forsake it, and must continue to aid it, as Ignatius himself rightly expected. "Therefore in him alone must be placed the hope that he will preserve and carry forward what he deigned to begin." If the Lord has helped us up to now, why will he not do so also in the future?

The Society is an institution and instrument of the apostolate. In these last years, while so many changes were taking place in order to adapt institutions and structures to current apostolic needs, I realized more clearly than ever the gifts of government that St. Ignatius had and his understanding, not only of the human person as such, but also of structures that must of necessity be flexible if one wants them to be effective and suited for all circumstances.

Looking at the Society in its true reality, I have been reminded often of what St. Francis Xavier wrote with such deep affection: "I don't know a better way to finish this letter than to protest to all the Society that, should I ever be forgetful of the Society of the name of Jesus, 'may my right hand wither' (Ps. 137:5), because I have come in so many ways to know how much I owe all in the Society."

2. The second love is of the church, the church of Christ, his spouse "with no speck or wrinkle or anything like that" that St. Ignatius spoke of perceptively as "our holy mother the hierarchical Church." Yes, this church, founded by Christ and having the Roman Pontiff as its visible head, to which we are bound by a special vow of obedience, "the principle and foundation of the Society."

With the passage of time and renewed experience one discovers such a serene and unchanging vigor in the church — a vigor flowing from Christ, its invisible head, and from the vitalizing action of his Spirit — that trust in it can only grow more firm. This is a trust that receives further confirmation when one encounters so many who, having separated themselves from the church, offer reasons that, at least apparently, seem to justify their attitude, but whom we subsequently find in a state of moral decline and atrophy as a result of being cut off from that movement of the Spirit that is uniquely characteristic of communion with the hierarchical church.

As life goes on and as you penetrate more deeply the mystery of the church and the charism of the Society, you grow aware with greater conviction that the true raison d'être of the Society lies in service of the church under the Roman Pontiff. To fail in this regard would be to sign our own death sentence. It is, rather, a reason for consolation to see how the Society endeavors always to be as faithful as possible to the spouse of Christ and to his vicar.

3. The third love is Jesus Christ, the Eternal King of the Exercises, the Incarnate Son of God, to whom we all owe a personal love, the key of our spirituality. Our deepest satisfaction and the source of every other satisfaction is to feel that Jesus Christ is the center of our life and our ideal. Christ who called me and directs me, who gives me his Spirit, who nourishes me with his flesh, who waits for me in the tabernacle, who shows me his pierced heart as the center and symbol of his love, who identifies himself with the hungry and the naked, with all the marginalized people of the world. Christ who comes to meet me on so many occasions of joy and of sorrow, as a close friend, who expects me, calls me, speaks to me: "The Master is here and wants to see you." Christ who said to St. Ignatius at La Storta: "I wish you to serve us." Without this love for Christ, the Society would no longer be the one that St. Ignatius founded, the Society of Jesus.

This love for Christ supposes and includes that for his Mother, "Our Lady," she who "places us with her Son," the Mother of the Society. Love for Mary: first taught me as a child, it has gone on growing throughout my life, without losing its childlike character, from the time when my mother died (I was ten years old) and my father said to me: "Pedro, you have lost a saintly mother, but you have another more saintly in heaven." There are moments and happenings in life that are not forgotten, the heritage of deeply good parents.

•

Thus, dear brothers, at the close of fifty years of life in the Society, the words of Ecclesiasticus come spontaneously to my lips: "I will give thanks to you, Lord and King, and praise you, God my savior, I give thanks to your name; for you have been protector and support to me" (Ecclus. 51:1–2). Moreover, I would like respectfully to ask of Our Lady that she let me borrow her words from the Magnificat: "My soul proclaims the greatness of the Lord and my spirit exults in God my savior; because he has looked upon his lowly servant" (Luke 1:46–48). Finally, I wish to finish with the prayer of St. Ignatius in his Spiritual Diary, spoken out of the depth of my weakness ("From the depth I call to you, Lord," Ps. 130:1): "Eternal Father, strengthen me; Eternal Son, strengthen me; Eternal Holy Spirit, strengthen me; Holy Trinity, strengthen me; my one God, strengthen me."

— "Three Models and Three Loves" in *RL* 1–10

TRUE BIOGRAPHY

Toward the end of his years as General of the Society of Jesus, Arrupe gave a series of interviews to a French Jesuit, Jean-Claude Dietsch. These were published in English under the title One Jesuit's Spiritual Journey. *When all the interviews were completed, Arrupe read the entire manuscript and wrote a brief conclusion for the book. The selection that follows, written in June 1981, is taken from that conclusion.*

In the life of each person there is an intimate dimension that cannot be communicated. Biographies are always unfinished portraits. In many matters, the light that is hidden within the depths of our being is lacking. If that light could be brought out, it would transform our image radically. But it cannot be imparted; its only value is in remaining hidden.

True biography is written only before the Lord. He alone is the one who can correct and add many things, sometimes those most precious elements which go unnoticed even by ourselves. Before the Lord, that is to say, as St. John of the Cross described it,

> In the blessed night
> hidden from others
> and looking at nothing
> without other guide or light
> than that which burns in the heart.

Someone has written, I don't know where, that the most interesting biography is that which is written "without ink." That remark can, doubtless, be applied to the preceding pages. It calls to mind especially the words of St. Paul to the Corinthians, "You are a letter from Christ, written not with ink, but with the Spirit of the living God" (2 Cor. 3:3).

I have the impression that my life is written in a single sentence: "It has unfolded according to the will of God." It is summed up in the words of Jesus, "Thy will be done" (Matt. 26:42). That can be said and written easily, but I myself do not understand either concretely or fully what it means. It is the mystery of all human life, which will only be revealed on the day when we see ourselves reflected in the face of God, when we shall find ourselves "face to face" with him (1 Cor. 13:12)

This does not mean that I consider my life to be especially extraordinary. The extraordinary thing is that, although I have been much lacking in what the orientation of my life should have been, the Lord continued to make possible his plan in my life. He loves us as we are, and he has loved me as I am. The miracle of life resides in this love which disposes, helps, and sustains. Marvelous things occur in everyone's life, and it is this same love of God which makes them appear as if they were our own doing, whereas in reality they are his work. One finds here all over again the great difficulty in marking the border between the human and the divine. — "Conclusion" in *OJ* 101–2

PRAYER FOR NEW EYES

Grant me, O Lord, to see everything now with new eyes,
to discern and test the spirits that help me read the signs
of the times,
to relish the things that are yours and to communicate
them to others.
Give me the clarity of understanding that you gave
Ignatius.

— "The Trinitarian Inspiration
of the Ignatian Charism," in *SL* 138

2

The Life of Christian Discipleship

Nowadays the world does not need words, but lives which cannot be explained except through faith and love for Christ poor.
— *Pedro Arrupe*

COMPANIONS OF JESUS

The center of Pedro Arrupe's life is Jesus Christ. He says this explicitly and witnesses to it indirectly over and over in his writings. This personal devotion to Jesus Christ supplies energy to his words and deeds, and solidity to his Gospel witness. Above everything else, it shaped his faith journey, lending unity to his countless everyday decisions. Thus, it lies behind every spiritual insight he endorsed, every exhortation he delivered to Christ's followers, and every hope he cherished for the consolation and redemption of our suffering world.

*In this opening section, the first set of selections gravitates around Arrupe's striking response to the question, **Who Is Jesus Christ?** He speaks with passion and energy. At the same time he indicates that genuine knowledge of Jesus flows from a rich* combination of "sources," including rigorous exegetical reflection, prayerful devotion, and the embodiment of that reflection and devotion in a praxis committed to justice. The fatherly advice found in **Friends of Jesus** and addressed to an audience of high school boys draws on the profound intimacy that Arrupe experienced in relationship with Jesus. The Jesuit General encourages these young believers to seek and nurture faith as the fruit of a real relationship. The third selection, **The Energy of Love,** is taken from one of Arrupe's homilies on the Sacred Heart of Jesus. It testifies to the link between the energy of prayer and the energy for action which authentic faith demands. **Following the Crucified Christ** comes from an address to Jesuits on the importance of the Spiritual Exercises. In it Arrupe touches the heart and notes the cost of Ignatius's Christ-centered mysticism: the call to follow Jesus leads to the foot of the cross in a world that crucifies. **Centered on Christ,** taken from Arrupe's formal letter to the Society of Jesus, "Our Way of Proceeding," reminds Jesuits that only the love of Christ can unify all the dynamic tensions that structure their vocation.

Who Is Jesus Christ?

This question was asked me, unexpectedly, during an interview which I gave on Italian television about five years ago. The question took me by surprise, and I answered it in a completely spontaneous way: "For me Jesus Christ is everything." And today I am giving you the same answer with still more strength and clarity. "For me Jesus Christ is *everything*." So, I would define what Jesus Christ represents in my life as "everything."

He was and he is my ideal from the moment of my entrance into the Society. He was and he continues to be my way; he was and he still is my strength. I don't think it is necessary to explain very much what that means. Take Jesus Christ from my life and everything would collapse — like a human body from which someone removed the skeleton, heart, and head.

•

It is true that the person of Jesus Christ is, from one point of view, very complex or, if you will, it presents multiple aspects. But in reality it is very simple: Whether Jesus Christ appears as a weak, fragile child or as the all-powerful; whether he is being affectionate with the little children or severe with the Pharisees, all is unified and rooted in one single aspect which is that of love; it is there that the person of Christ has a perfect unity and its greatest depth. What was for me, from the novitiate on, a simple intuition is enriched daily and has become very fruitful. And the heart of Christ as a symbol of this love has sustained me greatly in my life and has given me the key to understand the Lord without difficulty. Thus, this love gives life to everything else. Jesus Christ is a friend to me, especially in the Eucharist. Mass and prayer before the tabernacle nourish my thoughts and my activities.   — "Jesus Christ Is Everything" in *OJ* 37–38

•

To be a companion of Jesus — what does that mean today? First and foremost, it is to love Jesus Christ with all one's soul and, consequently, in a total and unconditional manner. Jesus Christ does not want half-hearted people among his companions. From that follows everything else. This companion, according to Ignatian terminology, is a person who, through love of Christ, is totally committed, under the standard of the cross, in the decisive struggle of our times for the faith and for the justice which that faith itself demands. There is no question, however, of a violent struggle, but of a commitment springing from love and charity. Thus, the faith is "informed" by charity and it manifests itself in works for humankind. As for justice, there is no question of the kind which by coldness can degenerate into an "unjust justice" — but of a justice well informed by charity, which is in reality a superior justice, a true justice which responds to the demands of love.

— "A Companion of Jesus" in *OJ* 41

Friends of Jesus

Would you like to have some good advice from me? Look upon Jesus as your friend, as your confidant. Learn to go and see him, to visit him, to "remain" with him, and you will see how many things you will learn. It is a wisdom which he alone can give you, the true knowledge which makes people wise, holy, and even happy. All that we need for our life is gradually attained with a pouring forth from heart to heart. "Tell me with whom you associate and I shall tell you who you are." If you go with Jesus, if you remain with Jesus, you will certainly become yourself another Jesus. Do you not recall that the principles of your association tell you that you should become personal friends of Jesus and that you should speak with him?

— "Eucharist and Youth" in *OA* 301

The Energy of Love

Today, when so many new sources of energy are being discovered, when we stand amazed at all the triumphs of scientific research in atomic physics and in the energy of the atom that may transform the whole universe, we do not sufficiently realize that all human power and natural energy is as nothing when compared with the superatomic energy of this love of Christ, who by giving his life vivifies the world. We, human beings that we are, can only transform already existing energy. But there exists an extraterrestrial source of energy which increases the energy of the world, an energy which has its source in the infinite love of Christ.

If we wish to transform this world of ours under its social and religious aspects, of the individual, the family, and society, here we have the only energy that can achieve this transformation. This is the infinite love of Christ which we acknowledge with St. Paul: "He loved and delivered himself for me" (Gal. 2:20).

— "What the Heart of Christ Means
to the Society" in *HA* 9

Following the Crucified Christ

Whoever wishes to follow Christ in glory has to follow him in humiliation and in sorrow. For the humanity to which we belong, and in which the divine Word became incarnate, is a sinful humanity, which dwells in a world beset with evil. It is not possible to disregard this or to release oneself from that situation. Only by accepting it such as it is, by confronting evil and struggling against sin, even to the cross and even to death, do we share in the redemption, for our own personal profit as well as for the good of all humankind.

Evil is an undeniable feature of our world. We can and ought to struggle against it always by trying to overcome it and convert it into a good of a higher order. But very often we make it worse, for ourselves and for our fellow human beings, by the very selfishness with which we pretend to escape from it. Called to love by the best part of our very nature, made by God to God's own image, called to a higher vocation of love by grace and the example of Christ, we humans, inherently low-spirited and cowardly, evade that call, withdraw within ourselves and, "wishing to gain all, lose all." Such is the drama of sin, present in human history from the beginning. Since their appearance upon the earth, humans are sinners.

The ascetical Christian tradition has never forgotten this. And it has understood that, for that reason, believers must turn ever anew to God by sincere conversion, from their condition as sinners. They have to struggle, inspired by grace, to bring about, in themselves and in others, the triumph of good over evil, of love over selfishness. But, above all, they must feel themselves identified with the death of Jesus, in which he offered himself to the Father in expiation for the sin of the world, that we might thus be reborn with him to new life.

— "The Jesuit and the Christ of the
Spiritual Exercises" in *OA* 269

Centered on Christ

Ignatian spirituality is eminently centered on Christ. Love for Christ gives unity to everything in the life and work of Ignatius, and in our way of proceeding, for everything is a concrete application of that love on the level of attitudes and actions. Just as everything converges on Christ, so the love for Christ, in Ignatius's intuition, unifies the dialectical pairs into which our apostolic action is diffracted:

- prayer and action;

- dedication to the perfection of self and neighbor;

- use of supernatural and human instruments;

- pluralism and unity;

- one's own effort and total dependence on God;

- poverty and having the most effective means;

- local insertion and universality.

To live that intense love for Christ the person, to aspire to a
"mind of Christ" that will make us be, seem, and act like him,
is the first and fundamental trait of our way of proceeding.

— "Our Way of Proceeding" in *SL* 74

EVANGELICAL POVERTY

*Issues surrounding evangelical poverty and the renewal of an
authentic spirit of poverty recur in Arrupe's letters and addresses. As part of the renewal demanded of the Society of Jesus
by the Second Vatican Council, Arrupe returns to the authentic
source of religious poverty: the call to follow Jesus found at the
heart of the Gospel. But this following can never be a matter of
the law only; it must flow from genuine intimacy with Christ
and a desire to follow him in everything. The first selection,*
Poverty Is a Gospel Mystery, *is taken from an address first given
to a group of Italian Jesuits in December 1973, but repeated in
a number of other countries during the period of preparation
for General Congregation 32. While addressed to Jesuits, these
reflections speak to all Christians, for all are called to embrace
the mysticism of evangelical poverty. In the second selection,*
Conscientization and Solidarity, *Arrupe draws on the thought
of the Brazilian educator Paulo Freire to name two key aspects
of the process by which a contemporary disciple grows into authentic poverty. This selection comes from a talk that Arrupe
gave in Rome and in other parts of the world after General
Congregation 32, reflecting the significance of the faith-justice
correlation that the Society of Jesus adopted in Decree 4, "Our
Mission Today." The universality of the call to embrace poverty becomes most explicit in the third selection,* **Poverty and
the Lay Christian.** *This address challenges Christians to see in
their call to follow the example of Christ an invitation to truly*

know God. For God, Arrupe writes, "is not only the God of the poor," but "in a real sense, God who is poor."

Poverty Is a Gospel Mystery

Poverty is a Gospel mystery, and one must love Christ to comprehend it. In the replies to my inquiry, one is struck by statements such as this: "There are those who simply do not know Christ's spirit of poverty, which is what makes one truly poor. Their living of poverty is not theological; it is not centered on Christ; and so it is merely an external, a material poverty." Such an attitude is obviously unacceptable and needs to be corrected with the help of prayer and an effort to acquire the proper spirit of the Exercises and the Constitutions.

The mystery of poverty springs from the mystery of the *kenosis* of Christ, Christ's emptying of himself. It is a mystery, something that human reason cannot fully comprehend, something we can approach only in the measure that we are enlightened by the Holy Spirit. The problematic of religious poverty is neither sociological nor financial. It is not even merely theological. It is a problematic of faith: of love for Christ poor, poor in the human life he chose for himself, poor in the life of his mystical body.

And so, to arrive at a measure of understanding of what poverty means, a double experience is necessary. A faith experience, first of all, of Christ's emptying of himself; but also a lived experience of being really poor. If either of these two experiences is lacking, one cannot really know what religious poverty is. If the mystical experience of Christ's *kenosis* is lacking, one might possibly know human poverty and misery — that poverty and misery which we are called upon to fight in themselves and in their effects — but one cannot know what religious poverty is and means. If the personal, lived experience of real poverty is lacking, one might possibly arrive at some knowledge of the poverty of the historical Christ and its characteristic traits, but one cannot know the actual poverty of the poor....

Faith impels us to the imitation of Christ poor, and this in turn impels us to actual poverty: such is the upward spiral generated by the interaction of faith experience and lived experience which is the basic pattern in this order of being. Interaction: for the lived experience of poverty impels us to the love of Christ, a love which purifies and liberates. As St. Ignatius puts it, "It is no small grace that the Divine Goodness gives us when it gives us the opportunity of actually tasting what we should always desire if we are to be conformed to our model Jesus Christ." ...

We all know how much St. Ignatius loved poverty. He looked on it as one of the basic virtues of the Jesuit apostle. Deriving this insight from interior illuminations of the Holy Spirit regarding the standard of the cross, he lost no time in translating it into practice: we are to love poverty as a mother and defend it as the rampart of religion.

Let us spell this out, using the same terminology that Ignatius does. What does poverty do? It disposes the human instrument to union with God and endows him or her with apostolic mobility. Union with God, effected by the theological virtues, is nourished by evangelical poverty, which is both founded in faith and increases faith, since Christ known by faith is the key to an understanding of what poverty really means, and poverty, in turn, is the supremely credible witness of what faith is: "faith without works is dead" (James 2:17).

Poverty means total detachment, at least in attitude; it means withdrawing trust from all things created and placing all our trust and all our hope in God, in the faith-certainty that our help can only come from him. It is to this total trust in the providence of God that poverty leads us by dispossessing us of everything and thus liberating us from attachment to anything. "The surest as well as the most needed contribution we can give to the reform of the universal church," says St. Ignatius, "is to go about it as lightly burdened with things as possible, as our Lord himself has shown us." The experience of human insecurity leads us to find shelter in the unfailing security of God....

We thus arrive at ultimate poverty: the giving up of everything, one's own self included, which imitates the *kenosis* of Christ. Rooted in the love of the Father, it is the highest degree of interior humility. To strip oneself in this way is to experience powerlessness in the presence of those who, having possessions, seem to have power. It is to experience humiliation, for to be poor is to be despised, to be cast aside, to be roughly treated.

In this connection, what a missionary must be ready to undergo in a foreign country is highly instructive. To find oneself alone in a great city, without a single friend or acquaintance, without provision of any kind, whether it be physical equipment or the support and security one derives from ordinary human relationships; to be poor even as far as language is concerned, unable to express oneself, to tell people what one is, what one knows; always to be in a position of inferiority, a child just learning to speak, contemptuously dismissed in every discussion, painfully aware of the poor impression one is always making, and of the pity, or else the hostility, with which one is regarded — all this brings home to a person better than empty theorizing what poverty, in the radical sense of *dis*-possession, really means. Not only does it take away external attachments, it makes one truly humble of heart; for to be poor is to be humiliated, and it is from humiliations that one learns humility.

This is one of the most valuable experiences we can acquire by living as the poor. The poor person has no rights in a society built on self-interest and the profit motive. The poor person is the one without a voice; the last in line; despised, ignored, forgotten. To understand the condition of the poor, it is necessary to experience it. If this experience is lacking, abstract theory and grand resolves are of little use.

— "Simplicity of Life" in *RL* 117–18, 120–22

Conscientization and Solidarity

To know thoroughly the reality that we meet or in which we live, we need more than a superficial glance at it in a random or purely formal contact, or a one-time experience of that reality. Knowing thoroughly means going beyond a mere spontaneous grasp to a critical understanding. Real conscientization (consciousness-raising) is a critical insertion in historical reality. That obliges one to accept the role of a subject who makes the world — or better, remakes it. It forces us to create our existence out of the material that life offers us. This is based, naturally, on the human capacity to work consciously on reality: hence conscientization necessarily includes the combination of our reflection on the world and our action on it.

It also follows from this that real conscientization has to be a process constantly in act, so that the new reality that is evolving can in turn be grasped in a new conscientization, which again will produce a still newer reality. It is an ongoing process; conscientization is always creative. "Thinking of the new reality as something untouchable is simplistic and reactionary, just as much as saying that the old reality was untouchable; if people, as working beings, continue to accept a 'made' world, they will very soon be plunged into a new darkness" (Paulo Freire).

And so, as conscientization increases, the manifestation of reality also increases, and the penetration of its phenomenological sense. If we merely contemplate the reality, we are no more than false intellectualists. Without the binomial action-reflection, there can be no conscientization; in other words, there can be no conscientization apart from practical action. The dialectical unity "action-reflection" will always be our most distinctive mode of being, our only effective way of changing the world.

There has to be, therefore, an insertion into reality and a reflection on reality. This double function enables us to know and act on reality, which in turn then acts on us. In other words, the external reality that we change then changes us in our very depths, and that very change makes us become "agents for change." This interaction is a manifestation and an effect of the intimate action of the Holy Spirit, who integrates, simultaneously and harmonically, the progress of a pilgrim humanity toward its true homeland and my growth in divine life that the Spirit communicates to me.

To know reality, to change our attitudes and achieve a true discernment, we must first be inserted into reality in an effective way. When I speak of insertion, I am referring to a real, critical insertion among the people of today, in order to create and shape society in an evangelical way.

A genuine insertion thus requires a change of personal attitude, the giving up, under many aspects, of our manner of being, thinking, and acting, so we can understand and come closer to the new realities that we want to evangelize. It is a real problem of life and experience, which gives us a special, profound, and realistic knowledge, which places us in solidarity with others, particularly with the poor and the weak....

This insertion or "incarnation" means solidarity with those who suffer, even to being identified with their lives. Here we find the most profound meaning of the poverty of the poor Christ, whom we want to imitate and follow. That phrase of the Exercises that describes our contemplation — "as if I were actually present" — takes on a vivid meaning that reflects the Gospel words: "What you did to the least of my brothers and sisters, you did to me" (Matt. 25:40). If we juxtapose St. Ignatius's two key lines from the Exercises — "What shall I do for Christ?" and "being poor with the poor Christ" — with those words of Christ — "What you did to the least of my brothers and sisters, you did to me" — everything takes on a new light, whose brilliance shakes our conscience. It is the apparition of Christ among the poor, his real presence among them.

> — "Some Far-Reaching Vistas of Decree 4
> of GC 32" in *JF* 147–50

Poverty and the Lay Christian

Here is matter for reflection not only for priests and religious, but also for lay men and women, particularly those who have been blessed by God with special abilities that can be of invaluable service to the community. It is mainly thanks to the gifts and talents received from God that they have achieved the economic and social position they now enjoy in society. They cannot in any way, therefore, use those gifts or that position to serve injustice, nor use them in an unjust way or only for their own comfort and advancement. Furthermore, they should seriously consider what they can personally do for those members of their community who are victims of injustice and particularly in need of their help and service. The talents and opportunities God has given us are an invitation to render personal service to Christ in our neighbor, particularly the oppressed, the poor, and the defenseless....

The human person must have a minimum of material goods in order to be. But it is not true that to *be* more we must always *have* more. We must learn to be "more" having "less."

We must learn what it is to have enough. This becomes more relevant today when an indiscriminate and selfish use of the world's resources by the richer nations threatens to cause irreparable damage to the essential elements of human life and to jeopardize the development of the poorer peoples.

Following the example of Christ, the church should be, above all, the church of the poor and the oppressed: the agricultural laborers, the refugees, those who suffer persecution for their faith, those deprived of basic human rights, those relegated by the powerful and prosperous to the margins of human society. We must, then, ask ourselves whether our way of life is such that all these people recognize in us the message of love and liberation which Christ brought to the world, whether they can find in the church hope and salvation.

The poor, the suffering, the disadvantaged, must stand at the very center of our concern. For they need justice as much as anyone else. Only they can neither buy it nor impose it. It was left for God to bring the good news to the poor.

But God is not only the God of the poor. God is, in a real sense, God who is poor. For the mystery of the incarnation has established a special relationship between God and poverty, the meaning of which goes much deeper than mere compassion. The Scriptures, especially the New Testament, invite us to plumb the depths of that meaning.

God is all-powerful. God has riches beyond our ability to estimate. But God is also a God of justice, who demands that justice be done. If, then, God, all-powerful and infinitely rich, identifies himself with the poor, it must be because the cause of the poor is somehow identified with the cause of justice.

Christ, the Son of God, empties himself, assumes the condition of a slave, and allows himself to be unjustly put to death. He does this, not because he tolerates injustice, or considers injustice unavoidable. On the contrary, one of the lessons we can learn from the cross is precisely to realize to what injustices our passion for wealth and power can lead. In Christ crucified we can see what we do to the poor when we are unjust to them. The cross shows the victims of injustice that Christ has made common cause with them, and that it is in him — God made human, God made poor, God put to death but risen from the dead — that they will find liberation, justice, and peace.

— "Witnessing to Justice" in *JF* 101, 102–3

DIMENSIONS OF
CHRISTIAN DISCIPLESHIP

As the General of the Society of Jesus during a period of profound change and renewal, Arrupe commented on virtually every aspect of Jesuit religious life at one time or another. While not everything he addressed would interest a wider audience, certain themes do manifest a kind of universal applicability, including the three topics addressed in this section. Although initially addressed to Jesuits, these selections speak to anyone interested in and called to live out a spirituality of active Christian discipleship.

The first selection, **In Service of Christ's Mission,** *draws on Pope Paul VI's encyclical* Ecclesiam suam *(1964) to address the relationship between vocation and mission, that is, between being a "disciple" called to follow Jesus and an "apostle" who is sent to serve others. The second set of four selections focuses on* **Discernment** *in relation to the themes of detachment, justice, conversion, and dialogue. The final set of selections in this section,* **The Society of Jesus and the Church,** *is taken from a conference that Arrupe gave in Rome on Ignatian Spirituality, and from his discussion of that conference in the interviews* *with Jean-Claude Dietsch. These reflections capture Arrupe's understanding of the Ignatian mysticism of ecclesial service, the Ignatian commitment to "think with the church," and the Jesuit's distinctive "fourth vow" of obedience to the pope.*

In Service of Christ's Mission

According to St. Ignatius, the "principle and foundation" of our life as Jesuits is the fourth vow, the vow of obedience to the Roman Pontiff with respect to missions. In other words, our life is based on mission, on being sent: the mission we receive from Christ, namely, of working in the service of the church through the mediation of the Roman Pontiff and the Society. Christ's command, "Go out to the whole world; proclaim the Good News to all creation" (Mark 16:15), we consider to be our mission from him, and rightly so.

Each one of us, at one time or another, has heard that call. Each has come to realize that, in responding to it, he is fulfilling a mission and thus giving to his life a depth of meaning which is both human and divine. For by so doing our life becomes, as it were, a prolongation of the intimate dialogue that begins within the Trinity, between the Father and the Word: "Here I am! I am coming to obey your will" (Heb. 10:7); the dialogue which expressed the love of the Father for fallen humanity, a love which the Son made known to us when he offered himself as victim on the cross: "What proves that God loves us is that Christ died for us while we were still sinners" (Rom. 5:8).

It is this same dialogue that is continued in the depths of our being when we hear the voice of the Word Incarnate inviting us to follow him: "You did not choose me; no, I chose you" (John 15:16); and we responded with generosity: "I offer my whole self to the task," and: "Lord, take and receive all my liberty."

The dialogue does not end there. It continues, this time between ourselves and the world that is not yet Christian. That world did not seek us; we sought it, on our own initiative. We showed it Christ, and we tried, we are trying, to convince it that in Christ there is no distinction between person and person, "no room for distinction between Greek and Jew, between the circumcised or the uncircumcised, between barbarian and Scythian, slave and free person" (Col. 3:11). A dialogue which is not only open to all, but also has nothing about it of compulsion: "Our mission is to proclaim what is unquestionably true and necessary for salvation; but we do not impose it by force.... We offer it as a saving gift, without infringement of either personal or civil liberty" (*Ecclesiam suam*).

We need patience to carry on this dialogue, for the dialogue of salvation was, on the whole, a gradual growth, starting from quite small beginnings and passing through successive stages of development before reaching complete success. So, too, our dialogue must take into account the slowness of the process by which human beings reach psychological and historical maturity, and await the hour when God will make it effective.

The dialogue then continues between the soul which does not yet believe and Christ himself. This is the final stage. The soul must now choose whether to accept or not, without reserve, Christ as God-made-human. The mystery of conversion: Christ's inward action on the soul, the soul's response.

First, then, the trinitarian dialogue; then Christ's dialogue with me, inviting me to give myself to him; then my dialogue with the world, with "souls," with unbelievers; and finally, the dialogue of the converted soul with Christ: this is the splendid sum and substance of our missionary activity.

If we thus reflect on our life in depth, we cannot but be consoled and strengthened by the realization that "the church is as much alive today as she ever was." And even though "all things considered, it seems that everything is still to do, and there is no end in sight to the work we begin today," we nevertheless perceive that "this is precisely the kind of ministry to which we are committed, and everything today urges us to carry it on with renewed vigor, vigilance, and intensity" (*Ecclesiam suam*).

Let us, then, look upon ourselves as sent by Christ "to make up all that has still to be undergone by Christ for the sake of his body, the church," as really and truly his helpers and fellow workers. The missionary is the bearer of hope to the world. Precisely at a time when the developed nations are caught up in the most serious ideological and social problems, and when the church herself seems to be passing through a period of trial and desolation, the ongoing work of the apostolate, with all it exemplifies of lively faith, supernatural outlook, persevering effort, and steady growth, is a ray of hope that gives new life and vigor to the true image of the church.

There is no doubt at all that the apostolic works being carried on in the nations or missions of the Third World are an inspiration to the rest of the world. The difficulties encountered, and the spirit in which they are encountered, are like a silent preaching of the word within the church herself. Thus, those who render service to the new churches render at the same time a witness that is both stimulus and encouragement to the whole church. It is not only the successes registered in the rising number of conversions; it is also the unremitting effort, amid hardships of every kind, of those who labor year after year without any tangible success, that compellingly testifies to the efficacious presence of the Spirit, and to the fact that God, who has been pronounced "dead" in societies reputed to be Christian, is very much alive.

It may be helpful to consider the missionary vocation as having this twofold aspect: it is a bringing of Christ to the world, and it is also an encountering of Christ in the world.

1. *Bringing Christ to the World.* It is clear that our missionary vocation has for its purpose to bring Christ to human beings and human beings to Christ. This requires of us a total acceptance of the totality of revelation, the deposit of faith in its entirety, so that we can proclaim to the world not yet Christian the whole truth and nothing but the truth. We achieve this total acceptance best of all by a process of "interiorization," so to speak, that is to say, by a vital contact with Christ at the deepest level of our being, the level at which he gives us to "really know God's secret, in which all the jewels of wisdom and knowledge are hidden" (Col. 2:2–3). This inward communication transforms us in a very real sense. It gives us a new form. It "Christifies" us — makes us other Christs — and that not only in our words, which, inspired by the Spirit of Christ, will be received as the words of Christ himself, but in our very lives, which, having taken on the form of Christ, will make us "Christ's incense to God for those who are being saved" (2 Cor. 2:15). This is the kind of tangible and trust-inspiring testimony that carries with it, in its turn, a transforming power. For when all is said and done, what transforms a person is not an ideology, not a theory, but life — something lived. A consecrated life, a life that continues in time the holocaust Christ offered once, will always be the definitive proof that what we teach is true.

2. *Meeting Christ in the World.* But the work of evangelization has another aspect which is often forgotten: that of discovering Christ and his Spirit in non-Christian societies and cultures.... One of our principal tasks today is to discover in other religions and in the traditions and ways of life of the peoples who do not know Christ, the signs that point to Christ.

To do this we must have a great love for those who "do not have the faith." We must regard them with understanding and sympathy, and treat them as equals always.

A lively personal interest will enable us to enter fully into the spirit of these cultures. By doing this, we will make our approach to them a highly constructive one, for we shall be enriching them with the fullness of Christ's message without antecedently destroying the values they already possess. Consider what a world of difference there is between these two attitudes: the attitude of those who enter the apostolate with utter self-assurance, as though they possessed all the truth that can possibly be known, failing to recognize or refusing to admit that they can learn a great deal from other nations and other cultures, that those nations and cultures can give them insights into our common humanity of which they are ignorant; and the attitude of those who approach these nations and cultures with sensitivity and respect, seeking to discern the work of the Spirit in cultural forms which may seem at first sight to be not only unfamiliar but unacceptable.

— "Missionary Vocation and Apostolate" in *RL* 59–63

Discernment

If the church is to fulfill her mission of witnessing to justice, she must practice discernment: that spiritual, supernatural discernment whereby one seeks, amid the complexities of any given situation, the direction in which the Holy Spirit, the Spirit of Truth, is leading.

Here, when we speak of the church practicing discernment, what we mean is that we — we, the people of God — must practice it. This discernment of what to do and how to act so that our very lives will bear witness to justice must now take place in the heart of every Christian, and at every level of community in

the church: the parish, the diocese, the episcopal conference, the
religious institute, the lay organization devoted to some form of
apostolic or social service.

•

There is an absolute prerequisite for the discernment of which
we speak. That prerequisite is conversion: the radical inner
transformation of a person which is sometimes referred to as
metanoia, a Greek word meaning "change of mind and heart."
Just what is conversion, *metanoia?* It is getting rid of something so that something else can take its place. It is getting rid
of everything that prevents us from being filled with the Holy
Spirit; from being completely at the disposal of that Spirit which
Jesus promised to send, "the Spirit of truth who issues from the
Father, and who is to be Jesus' witness," leading us, who are
also called to be his witnesses, to "the complete truth" (John
15:26–27, 16:13).

This is why there can be no true discernment without conversion. For discernment, when all is said and done, is nothing
else but being guided by the Spirit: seeing the world, and what
we must be and do in the world, no longer with our own eyes,
but with the eyes of the Spirit.

Conversion, then, is a change, a change that takes place deep
inside us, a radical change. Let us make no mistake about it:
there is nothing superficial about conversion. It is not, for instance, deciding, after a somewhat more fervent retreat, to "give
something to the poor," or to be a little more generous to one's
"favorite charity." This is a praiseworthy thing in its way, but
it is not conversion.

Conversion is not a giving away of something that we can
well afford to lose. It goes much deeper than that. It is a
putting away of something that we are: our old self, with its all-
too-human, all-too-worldly prejudices, convictions, attitudes,

values, ways of thinking and acting; habits which have become so much a part of us that it is agony even to think of parting with them, and yet which are precisely what prevent us from rightly interpreting the signs of the times, from seeing life steadily and seeing it whole.

Conversion, in short, is divesting ourselves of what St. Paul calls the "old person" in order to put on the "new person": the person in Christ Jesus; the person who has accepted the Gospel without any reservations and stands ready to do whatever it may require of him or her; the "Third Class of Human Beings" of the Exercises of St. Ignatius, that is, one who has reached that degree of detachment from all one has and is that one is prepared to keep or not keep them, use them or not use them, only as it shall be to the greater service and praise of the divine majesty.

•

Let us examine our attitude toward those who differ in opinion from us. Is it open or closed? While taking all prudent measures to preserve the purity and integrity of our faith, do we at the same time allow for that measure of freedom in research, reflection, and discussion whereby our human understanding of revealed truth is enriched and the right practical decisions arrived at with regard to contingent, ever-changing situations?

If, after all this, we still find that a difference of opinion exists among us, we should try to resolve it by the dialectic of Christian dialogue. St. Ignatius suggests a form of this dialectic worth considering:

> Every good Christian ought to be more ready to give a favorable interpretation to another's perhaps obscure statement or position than to condemn it. But if he can find no way at all to defend the other's statement made

or position taken, let him make careful inquiry into what
the other means by it. And if the latter's attitude or
understanding of the matter seems to be somewhat unreasonable, let him gently and courteously point this out to
him. And if this course of action brings no result, let him
try all other suitable ways to help the other see things in
proper perspective and without misconceptions.

— "Witnessing to Justice" in *JF* 93, 94–95, 99

The Society of Jesus and the Church

Service is the key idea of the charism of Ignatius. It is an idea
whose moving power achieved in the life and spirituality of
Ignatius — even in his mystical phase — a total realization: un-
conditioned and limitless service, service that is large-hearted
and humble. It could be said that even the trinitarian "lights"
which enriched his mystical life, rather than leading to a passive and contemplative quieting, spurred him to a greater
service of this God he contemplated with such great love and
reverence.

With the inevitability with which an idea that has taken
strong hold of one manifests itself in deeds and communicates
itself to those close to one, Ignatius passed on to his first companions this mysticism of service. Nadal will say, "The Society
walks along the path of the Spirit. It struggles for God under
the standard of the cross. It serves the Lord alone and the
church, his bride, under the Roman Pontiff, the vicar of Christ
on earth."

The embodiment of this service in concrete form is the object of an interesting evolution that covers the entire period of
the life of Ignatius from his conversion up to the point when
his charism stands fully defined in the founding moments of the

Society.... The whole history of the Society, which is the unfolding of the Ignatian intuition in the course of the centuries, finds no better one-word synthesis than that of "service."

•

The Ignatian vision of the church is supernatural. In his mystical experience, Ignatius reached the point of glimpsing the mystery of the church, which became one of the principal teachings of the Second Vatican Council. He proposes the church to us in the first place as the bride of Christ, vivified and guided by the Spirit of Christ. And it is on this that the fundamental attitude of a Christian is based. He sees it also as a mother, a virgin mother, who "raises up to a new and immortal life children conceived of the Holy Spirit and born of God." The expression "our holy mother the church" is the one that we hear most frequently issuing from his lips. But, given his practical and apostolic purpose, the church that he has in mind here is not that triumphant church, the heavenly Jerusalem, but the "church militant," the church on pilgrimage in this world, and this church not only in its spiritual or charismatic aspect, but also in its visible and institutional aspect. For this reason he does not forget to speak of it, one time or other, as the "hierarchical church."

Finally, the church considered here by St. Ignatius is not at all an ideal church, nor the primitive community of Jerusalem, but the church as it has gone on developing over the course of history, the church of his time, that of Stations, of indulgences and of lighted candles and, we can add, the church before the Council of Trent, with its abuses, its ignorant clergy, its absentee bishops, its worldly popes and cardinals.

In this church that is militant, hierarchical, and contemporary, St. Ignatius tells us, we ought to have a "sound sentiment," we ought to form correct and orthodox opinions. It has been rightly observed that in the language of St. Ignatius the words "sentiment" and "form an opinion" have a very rich meaning. This is not a matter of simple intellectual knowledge. It is a knowledge that is imbued with affectivity — the fruit of spiritual experience — that energizes the whole person. There is here a "sentiment" that is "fostered in the church." The thinking is of a member of the mystical body who lives the divine life of the church, and thus is in harmony with the thinking of the church itself. This sense of the faithful (*sensus fidei*) is a gift that the Holy Spirit pours into the spirit of a Christian. Thus it is not out of the ordinary to find simple, uneducated persons who possess it in a high degree.

— "Ecclesial Service" in *RL* 254–55, 269–70

•

The vow of obedience to the Sovereign Pontiff — our fourth vow — and the spirit of this vow constitute for St. Ignatius the origin and foundation of the Society of Jesus. This is why this vow and its spirit pervade all our *Constitutions* as well as our spirituality. This vow, therefore, ought to be carefully interpreted. We should be aware of the obligations that it implies and the spirit it engenders. There are some persons who think that, from a strictly juridical point of view, it concerns only "the sending on a mission." Others think that it has a wider import. I, for my part, think that it has a wider import. The Holy Father is the highest Superior of the Society, and all the doctrine of obedience established by St. Ignatius ought to be applied to him. And that should be done with the greatest sincerity. The Holy Father represents Jesus Christ. We ought to love him, we ought to defend him, and we ought to study and explain his doctrine.

That certainly does not prevent us from having also, according to St. Ignatius, the duty of "representation" with all its conditions. For example, the "representation" is not necessarily public, especially with the mass media, which tend to transform all "representation" into a spectacle or an opposition. Our obedience is not passive. We have the availability of free persons. But it is true that, as Jesuits, once all the representations are made, we practice evangelical obedience. It is Jesus Christ who, by his vicar and the superiors of the Society, sends us. This is the basic apostolic dimension. Everything comes in here: trinitarian love, fidelity to Christ, love of the church, discernment, availability, mobility, loyalty; such is the Ignatian concept.

— "The Fourth Vow" in *OJ* 93

THE SACRED HEART OF JESUS

As a boy Pedro Arrupe developed a devotion to the Sacred Heart of Jesus. As a Jesuit this love grew. Indeed, the devotion to the Sacred Heart, so closely associated with the Jesuit saint Claude La Colombière, has long been cherished and promoted by the Society of Jesus. However, in the decades before and after the Second Vatican Council, fervor for this devotion and others like it began to erode in many parts of the world. With a profound reverence for the Sacred Heart as a religious symbol, yet sensitive to those who no longer found it inspiring as a religious devotion, Arrupe set out to reinterpret the symbol and revitalize the devotion. Many of his addresses, letters, homilies, and personal reflections on the topic have been published in a collection entitled In Him Alone Is Our Hope: Texts on the Heart of Christ. *The four selections included here evoke Arrupe's mystical intuitions about and theological insights into this profound devotion.*

The Word

The word "heart," both in everyday language and in biblical terminology, is one of those words which Karl Rahner has called an *Urwort,* that is, a root-word, a parent-word which generates other words. Such words are packed with meaning and are very difficult to define, and for that reason are also highly evocative. Just as a small sea conch conjures up the roar and fury of the sea, such words stir up a rich variety of ideas and sentiments. The word "mother" is another example. Who can say all that this word evokes? Or who can reduce it to a definition? To any definition of this word one can say "yes, all that but more," because no one can reach the very depth of its meaning and even less communicate it to others. The value of these words is precisely that we can understand each other's meaning when we refer to deep and complex realities. The psychology of language has in such words a subject for absorbing research.

But the very richness and depth of these words is, in part, their weakness. They are used so much in human communication that they become victims of abuse and end up cheapened and corrupted, or else they are watered down so that they lose their flavor, or again they are inflated and adapted to the fleeting fancy of the current vogue, and then discarded abruptly. Fortunately nature always wins out, and these words — which instead of a human figment seem to be a divine gift — come to life again and bloom, their profound meaning and values intact.

"Heart of Jesus" is an expression that has suffered such vicissitudes. Marked with the symbolism and with the literary style and imagery of an era — which is necessarily fleeting — it seemed that it would remain buried beneath the wave of renewal. Not for long. "Heart of Christ" is a phrase of unusual aptness and so rooted in biblical meaning that it is irreplaceable. It was sufficient to free it of superficial connotations for the original, rich, and mysterious meaning to be restored. Heart of Jesus: all the love of Christ, God and human, sent by the Father, through the Spirit, who offers himself in redemption for all and, with each of us, establishes a personal relationship.

— "The Heart of Christ" in *HA* 68–69

The Complete Christ

The person of Christ comes to be known only when he is known in all the riches of his heart, which on the one hand is the symbol of his love, and on the other has been the material organ that has beaten with the human love of Christ for others. This knowledge of Christ is the basis of all knowledge. And Christ, who is the way, the truth, and the life, has to be known under this meaningful image, which can be discovered in each page of the Gospel when we read it at leisure.

This image is sublime, immense, infinite. It takes many shapes. There is the lovable Christ who embraces little children, the Christ who denounces and castigates the hypocritical Pharisees, the Christ who commands the angry winds and tempestuous waves to be still, the Christ whose divine attributes seem to fade away and vanish in the dark hours of Gethsemane, the Christ who speaks with the greatest simplicity and utters at the same time the "most sublime teachings, which no one can ever fully comprehend in their fathomless profundity."

And when we try to find the reason of this authenticity and unmatched uniqueness of Christ, we discover that there is an exceptional aspect in this figure. He is the savior. Every page in the Gospel unravels the mysterious process of salvation through this exalted and divine person.

Christ is the savior because he saved us, each one of us. "He loved me and he delivered himself for me" (Gal. 2:20). But if we search the Gospels for the ultimate reason of the love that throbs in each of their pages, we shall find a further and much deeper reason. This love of Christ for all people has a profounder trinitarian source: the love of the Word for his Father.

It could be said that every line of the Gospel, every word of it, is throbbing with the boundless love of Christ, who is burning with love for each human being and desires to ransom each of them in order to give glory to his eternal Father.

To the question whether this is the complete picture of Christ, the answer is in the negative. Because Christ delivered himself for us, he laid down his life for us, but he rose from the dead. And Christ today is a living person. Where is he? He is at the right hand of the Father, interceding on our behalf, and in the tabernacle, the eucharistic Christ. And searching for the reason of this intercession in heaven and of this real presence in the Blessed Sacrament, we find it to be no other than the infinite love of Christ for us, with whom he wishes to abide for all time.

Does, therefore, this historical Christ, this risen and glorious Christ, this eucharistic Christ, sum up the entire personality of Christ? Augustine gives us the answer, and it is no. "If you wish to love the whole Christ, you must open your heart wide. For Christ, as the head, is in heaven at the right hand of the Father, but his presence extends to the whole world in his members, that is, in each human being."

Nor is that all. We know that the one and only person that is in Christ, that is, the Word of God, dwells in the innermost depths of our heart. This truth provokes St. Bernard's question: "Where is the one who speaks from the most hidden recesses of our soul? Which way did he enter? Did he enter through the

eyes? Or was it through the ears or touch?" And the saint supplies the answer: "None of these ways, because this presence is something of my own intimate being." This which is my innermost self has been within me from the very first moment of my existence. It needed no door through which to enter. This divine Word, which dwells in the depths of my soul and speaks to me, is also the person of Christ. This is the complete Christ, the infinite love, symbolized in that heart, which wishes to identify itself with us.　　　— "What the Heart of Christ Means
to the Society" in *HA* 6–7

The Humanity of Christ

The objective value of the Sacred Heart devotion is taught clearly in many documents of the church and the Society. It would be very difficult to maintain, and even more difficult to justify scientifically, the opinion that the fundamentals of this devotion are outdated or lack a theological basis, if one presents in its essentials the message which it offers and the response which it demands.

Christ, fully divine and fully human, precisely by virtue of being the incarnate Son of God, possesses all genuinely human values in their fullness. He is God, and at the same time, the most human of human beings. In his person he embodies love in its fullest measure, because it expresses the Father's gift to us of his Son incarnate, and because it is in itself the perfect synthesis of his love for the Father and of his love for all people.

It is this mystery of divinely human love, symbolized in the heart of Christ, that the traditional Sacred Heart devotion has endeavored to express, and which it has sought to emphasize, in a world ever more eager for love, ever more in need of comprehension and justice. Between the word of God and the pierced heart of Jesus Christ on the cross lies the whole humanity of the

Son of God, and the eclipse of sound theological understanding of that humanity has been one of the reasons which has led to the depreciation of the heart as symbol. To bypass the total humanity of Christ means to leave a theological vacuum between the symbol and the object symbolized, a vacuum which anthropomorphism and pietism are always ready to fill. To neglect the humanity of Christ means, above all, to lose the communitarian and consequently the ecclesial dimension of a Christ-centered spirituality.

The church is born of the incarnation. Indeed, it is a continuing incarnation. It is the mystical body of God made human. Hence there is nothing less individualistic than a genuine love of Christ: the very concept of reparation proceeds from an authentic communitarian demand, that of the mystical body.

Overcoming the psychological obstacles which the external forms of this devotion may present, the Jesuit should revitalize it with the solid and robust Christ-centered spirituality of the Exercises which, integrally Christ-centered and culminating in total commitment, prepare us to "feel" the love of the heart of Christ giving unity to the whole Gospel. The life of the Jesuit is perfectly integrated in his response to the call of the Eternal King and in the "Take, O Lord, and receive" of the Contemplation for Obtaining Love, which is the crown of the Exercises. To live that response and that offering will be for each one of us and for the whole Society the true realization of the spirit of Ignatian consecration to the heart of Christ.

From this intense living of the Spirit of the Exercises issues, with a certain inescapable apostolic urgency, the pledge to live and offer one's own prayer and work in union with the heart of Christ and so attain to a life profoundly centered in Christ and the church. The Apostleship of Prayer has long animated, and still continues to animate, the priestly perspective of many

Christian lives, drawing them onward to the eucharistic sacrifice of Christ and the consecration of the world to God. This instrument of the Apostleship of Prayer, which has so greatly helped the People of God in the past, can with appropriate renovation and adaptation, render new and greater service today, when the need is so keenly felt to establish apostolic groups of prayer and earnest spiritual commitment.

— "Facing a New Situation: Difficulties and Solutions" in *HA* 15–17

The Divine-Human Harmonics of Love

The reason for loving one's neighbor is a theological reason which closely relates it to the love of God. They are not two parallel loves, nor is love of neighbor a subordinate love. It is the two sides of one love, as one is the love within the Trinity and one the love with which Christ loves the Father and humankind. The close connection of the second commandment to the first (as we shall see later, in Paul's and John's description it acquires its highest expression) conforms to this profound causality: one cannot love God without loving one's brother and one's sister, and he who for God loves his brothers and sisters is already loving God (cf. Mark 5:45 and Luke 6:35).

The three synoptic Gospels report instances when Christ likens love of neighbor to love of God. In Matthew (22:34–40) and in Mark (12:28–34), Christ answers the Pharisee's provocative question and with a hint of challenge he blends both commandments into one. In Luke (10:25ff.) it is a quibbling lawyer who has to respond to Christ's sparring question. The casuist links the precept in Deuteronomy (6:5) about the love of God with that of Leviticus (19:8) about the love of one's neighbor — neighbor of course, as the lawyer understands the word. To correct the notion, Jesus tells him the parable of the Good Samaritan (Luke 10:29–37).

Of nothing else did Christ speak so much as of love, with the exception perhaps of the kingdom: "the kingdom of heaven is like...." But even the parables of the kingdom are set in a context of love. Love, with all its harmonics (friendship, compassion, tolerance, benevolence, mercy, sadness, hope, joy, etc.), is enough to describe Christ in his inner self, in his heart. Christ calls his followers to goodness and love, sometimes directly, from the beatitudes right up to the sermon of the last supper, and at other times indirectly and through sublime allegories — the prodigal son, the lost pearl, the stray sheep and the whole cycle of the Good Shepherd parables. Christ "goes about doing good" (Acts 10:38) and displays his miraculous power in "signs" which are more often acts of kindness than proofs of his messiahship.   — "The Heart of Christ" in *HA* 77–78

PRAYER TO CHRIST OUR MODEL

Arrupe concludes his letter entitled "Our Way of Proceeding" with a prayer addressed to Christ as model and "way." This prayer draws heavily on Scripture and the vision of Ignatius. It takes the form of an intercession modeled after one of the most sublime suggestions that Ignatius sets out in the Second Week of the Spiritual Exercises: "Here it will be to ask for an interior knowledge of Our Lord, who became human for me, that I may love him more intensely and follow him more closely."

Lord, meditating on "our way of proceeding," I have discovered that the ideal of *our* way of acting is *your* way of acting. For this reason I fix my eyes on you; the eyes of faith see your face as you appear in the Gospel. I am one of those about whom

St. Peter says: "You did not see him, yet you love him, and still without seeing him, you are already filled with a joy so glorious that it cannot be described, because you believe" (1 Pet. 1:8).

Lord, you yourself have told us: "I have given you an example to follow" (John 13:15). I want to follow you in that way so that I can say to others: "Be imitators of me as I am of Christ" (1 Cor. 11:1). Although I am not able to mean it as literally as St. John, I would like to be able to proclaim, at least through the faith and wisdom that you give me, what I have heard, what I have seen with my eyes, what I have contemplated and touched with my hands concerning the Word of Life; the Life manifested itself, and I have seen it and give witness (1 John 1:1). Although not with bodily eyes, certainly through the eyes of faith.

Above all, give me that *sensus Christi* about which St. Paul speaks (1 Cor. 2:16): that I may feel with your feelings, with the sentiments of your heart, which basically are love for your Father and love for humankind. No one has shown more charity than you, giving your life for your friends with that *kenosis* of which St. Paul speaks (Phil. 2:7). And I would like to imitate you not only in your feelings but also in everyday life, acting, as far as possible, as you did.

Teach me your way of relating to disciples, to sinners, to children, to Pharisees, Pilates, and Herods; also to John the Baptist before his birth and afterward in the Jordan. Teach me how you deal with your disciples, especially the most intimate: with Peter, with John, with the traitor Judas. How delicately you treat them on Lake Tiberius, even preparing breakfast for them! How you washed their feet!

May I learn from you and from your ways, as St. Ignatius did: how to eat and drink; how to attend banquets; how to act when hungry or thirsty, when tired from the ministry, when in need of rest or sleep.

Teach me how to be compassionate to the suffering, to the poor, the blind, the lame, and the lepers; show me how you revealed your deepest emotions, as when you shed tears, or when you felt sorrow and anguish to the point of sweating blood and needed an angel to console you. Above all, I want to learn how you supported the extreme pain of the cross, including the abandonment of your Father.

Your humanity flows out from the Gospel, which shows you as noble, amiable, exemplary and sublime, with a perfect harmony between your life and your doctrine. Even your enemies said: "Master, we know that you are truthful, that you teach the way of God in truth and care not for anyone's opinion, for you regard not a person's status" (Matt. 22:16). The Gospel shows your virile manner, hard on yourself in privations and wearying work, but for others full of kindness, with a consuming longing to serve.

It is true that you were hard on those who acted in bad faith, but your goodness drew the multitudes; the sick and infirm felt instinctively that you would have pity on them; you so electrified the crowds that they forgot to eat; with a knowledge of everyday life you could offer parables that everyone understood, parables both vigorous and esthetic. Your friendship was for everyone, but you manifested a special love for some, like John, and a special friendship for some, like Lazarus, Martha and Mary. Show me how you expressed joy at festive gatherings; for example, at Cana.

You were in constant contact with your Father in prayer and your formal prayer, often lasting all night, was certainly a source of the luminous transcendence noticed by your contemporaries. Your presence instilled respect, consternation, trembling, admiration, and sometimes even profound fear from various types and classes of people.

Teach me your way of looking at people: as you glanced at Peter after his denial, as you penetrated the heart of the rich young man and the hearts of your disciples.

I would like to meet you as you really are, since your image changes those with whom you come into contact. Remember John the Baptist's first meeting with you? And the centurion's feeling of unworthiness? And the amazement of all those who saw miracles and other wonders? How you impressed your disciples, the rabble in the Garden of Olives, Pilate and his wife, and the centurion at the foot of the cross.

The same Peter who was vividly impressed by the miraculous catch of fish also felt vividly the tremendous distance between himself, a sinner, and you. He and the other apostles were overcome with fear.

I would like to hear and be impressed by your manner of speaking, listening, for example, to your discourse in the synagogue in Capernaum or the Sermon on the Mount, where your audience felt you "taught as one who has authority" and not as the Scribes (Matt. 7:29).

In the words of grace that came from your mouth the authority of the Spirit of God was evident. No one doubted that the superhuman majesty came from a close bond between Jesus and God. We have to learn from you the secret of such a close bond or union with God: in the more trivial, everyday actions, with that total dedication to loving the Father and all humanity, the perfect *kenosis* at the service of others, aware of the delicate humanity that makes us feel close to you and of that divine majesty that makes us feel so distant from such grandeur.

Give me that grace, that sense of Christ, your very heartbeat, so that I may live all of my life, interiorly and exteriorly, proceeding and discerning with your spirit, exactly as you did during your mortal life.

Teach us your way so that it becomes our way today, so that we may come closer to the great ideal of St. Ignatius: to be companions of Jesus, collaborators in the work of redemption, each one of us an *alter Christus*.

I beg Mary, your Most Holy Mother who contributed so much to your formation and way of acting, to help me and all sons of the Society to become her sons, just like you, born of her and living with her all the days of your life.

— "Our Way of Proceeding" in *SL* 79–82

3

Ignatius Loyola

Ignatius was a man who had received from God the special
grace of grasping the mystical quintessence of the Gospel.
— *Pedro Arrupe*

THE MYSTICAL EXPERIENCES OF
IGNATIUS LOYOLA

*Arrupe's prayers, letters, and spiritual writings continually echo
the mysticism and holiness of his "father in faith," St. Ignatius
Loyola. Yet his is a distinctive echo, a contemporary reception,
not a merely literal replication of Ignatius's words and insights.
As the General commissioned by Vatican II to initiate a renewal
of the order, Arrupe occupies a singular place among contemporary commentators on the Ignatian vision. His way of reading
the life of Ignatius, the Spiritual Exercises, and the dynamics of
the Jesuit vocation guided the Society's response to the Council
and stimulated a renaissance in Ignatian spirituality. Hence, the
key events in the life of Ignatius function as primary terms in
Arrupe's spiritual lexicon, while Arrupe's reflections on Ignatius
shed new light on the depth and impact of the latter's mystical*

heritage. In all, Arrupe's way of reading the Ignatian heritage provides new access to the riches of that tradition today.

The five selections in the first section follow in a general way the chronology of Ignatius's mystical journey. In the first, **Ignatius's Conversion,** *Arrupe reflects on the interior pilgrimage that unfolded while Ignatius was convalescing from injuries he received during a military battle in Pamplona, a story told in Ignatius's own* Autobiography. *Arrupe interprets this foundational spiritual event not as a conversion to "service as an ideal," but a conversion to "the one Lord worthy of that service." Significantly, he utilizes the story of Ignatius to introduce his 1979 address to the General Assembly of the Worldwide Federation of Christian Life Communities, a lay movement that takes its inspiration from the Ignatian charism.*

The next three selections come from Arrupe's brilliant theological essay "The Trinitarian Inspiration of the Ignatian Charism." Here he reflects at some length on three places where Ignatius experienced the defining mystical graces of his life, places whose names function as code words in Ignatian spirituality and Jesuit religious life: Manresa, the Cardoner, and La Storta. The cave at **Manresa** *is intrinsically linked with Ignatius's classic work,* The Spiritual Exercises. *Over a period of ten months spent largely in intense prayer and fasting, Ignatius submitted himself to the mystical pedagogy that gave rise to an entirely distinctive current in the history of Christian mysticism, the spirituality associated with his name. The particular mystical experience that comes to be associated with* **the Cardoner River** *took place during the time in Manresa. Ignatius spoke of it not as a vision but an unsurpassable "illumination." So intense was that grace, Ignatius tells us, that he saw more in that one experience than in all the experiences of the rest of his life put together. Years later, in the chapel of* **La Storta** *on the outskirts of Rome, while traveling with two of his first companions, Diego Laínez and Pierre Favre, Ignatius experienced the vision that gave definitive shape and a name to the Society of Jesus. In it he saw God the Father placing him with Christ carrying his cross. For Ignatius, this not only confirms but deepens the call he received years before while standing on the banks of the Cardoner: to follow Jesus, who embraces suffering in order to overcome it. Arrupe will return to La Storta over and over in his writings and offer his last "unspoken" homily as General of the Society of Jesus in the chapel of La Storta (see p. 203).*

*The final selection in this section, **Ignatius in Rome,** comes from Arrupe's last major work on Ignatian spirituality, "Rooted and Grounded in Love." His focus here is on the example of Ignatius (now the first General of the Society of Jesus) living in Rome, directing the explosive growth of the new congregation, writing the* Constitutions, *yet all the while attentive to those who suffer. Ignatius finds and follows Jesus by acting on behalf of the poor of the city. Arrupe examines the mystical roots of this Ignatian generosity, this willingness to be "interrupted" by the sufferings and needs of others.*

Ignatius's Conversion

From his earliest years, the idea of service came as naturally to Ignatius as the air we breathe. Everything he saw in the ancestral home of Casa-Torre spoke to him of service — the pursuits of his brothers, his family traditions, the service of "serfdom" given by the peasants as they worked and tilled the fields, the service of "loyal servants" rendered by members of his own family to their faraway Lord, whom one helped in time of war and who rewarded this faithful service in time of peace.

When he was barely fifteen, Ignatius entered the service of an important member of the court, the royal treasurer, and followed him for ten years. At his death, Ignatius passed into the service of the duke of Najera, viceroy of Navarre, and from there he moved into the royal service, until, four years later, he fell wounded on the walls of Pamplona.

As a result of his own experiences, Ignatius's concept of service was a knightly one that included honor, fidelity, courage, and the desire for glory. The books of knight-errantry which he enjoyed reading were the embodiment of such ideals.

In the course of his convalescence, when he thought of a certain lady, "who had taken such a hold on his heart," his love still expresses itself in terms of service: "he imagined what he would do in the service of a certain lady, . . . the verses, the words he would say to her, the deeds of arms he would do in her service." For Ignatius, to love was to serve.

Ignatius's conversion led him, not to give up the ideal of service, but to find a new "Lord." During the first phase of his conversion, he had in mind to serve the Lord in a way that was still rather worldly — not to say belligerent and competitive! — "St. Francis did this, therefore I have to do it." It is only later, through a graced masterpiece of introspection and discernment, that he takes apart and analyzes all the different elements that have combined to form his ideal. Ignatius purifies his idea of service and then proceeds to build his whole spirituality on the foundation of this purified concept — which becomes the first principle and foundation of the Exercises: "Human beings are created to praise, reverence, and serve God our Lord."

For Ignatius, service of the Creator is axiomatic — there is simply no call to justify or prove it. It is the natural condition of "the creature": he is created "for," that is to say, for a purpose which binds him to the One who gives him his very existence. Two elements of service progressively develop in the dynamic of the Exercises: service in love (the final contemplation in the Exercises is precisely aimed at seeking this love), and the person one serves out of love: God, the divine majesty, the Three Divine Persons, Christ in his incarnation, in his life, his passion, and in the glory of his resurrection.

All the Exercises will be based on the concept of service in one way or another, the words "service" or "to serve" will appear fifty times. Even Christ's relationship to the Father is seen as one of service. For Ignatius, the service of God is the criterion for discernment in the ordering of one's life. "The reason the retreatant wants or retains anything will be solely the service, honor, and glory of the Divine Majesty." Service is an unconditional attitude. "The retreatant should enter upon the Exercises with magnanimity and generosity toward his Creator and Lord, and offer him his entire will and liberty, that his Divine Majesty may dispose of him and all he possesses according to his most holy will." This service of God disposes the retreatant "for the way in which he can better serve God in the future."

However, the ideal of service is most fully and clearly expressed in the center point of the Exercises — the Call of the Earthly King, the introduction to the consideration of different states of life, the Two Standards. Ignatius's best memories of his knightly ideas are recalled here. "If anyone would refuse the invitation of such a king, how justly he would deserve to be condemned by the whole world and looked upon as an ignoble knight." And he continues: "those who wish to give greater proof of their love, and to distinguish themselves in whatever concerns the service of the Eternal King and Lord of All" will want to imitate Christ humble and poor, for his "greater service and praise."

The last part of the Exercises closes with the idea of service, but with a certain tone that is quite different from the First Principle and Foundation, where the word "love" is not mentioned:

"The zealous service of God our Lord out of pure love should be esteemed above all."

> — "A World Community at the Service
> of One World" in *OA* 227–29

Manresa

When Ignatius, "so as not to be recognized," withdraws to the isolated Manresa, he brings as his spiritual baggage only the firm decision to make a radical change of life, a determination to expiate his sins — such is the nature of his asperities, vigils, and extenuating hours of prayer — and the desire for light to guide his new life. He will also "note down certain things in a book that he carefully carried with him and by which he was greatly consoled." This is the Ignatius who is reflective and methodical by nature. His natural qualities crystallize and take on new forms and expressions: absolute coherence between his thinking and his life, a will of iron, a singular capacity for introspection and analysis.

The first four months of the eleven he will stay at Manresa are a desert across which blows a fire that purifies his past: penances, vigils, a deliberately slovenly and repulsive exterior and, above all, a surrender to prayer. He lives this spiritual maceration "in a state of great and constant happiness, without having any knowledge of the inward things of the spirit." It is the destruction of the carnal and mundane self of which he will speak in the Exercises. There follows a *second period* of inner turbulence, during which the resistance of his body and his spirit reach a crisis. Is this sort of life bearable? What is the value of it, if the obsession with his past and present sins continues? It is a time of scruples and temptations, even of suicide. But it is also the beginning of "great changes in his soul...that he had never experienced before." His capacity for introspection, for discernment, will save him. "From the lessons God had given him he now had some experience of the diversity of spirits." Consolation and desolation come upon him, one after the other.

Then the *third phase* of his stay at Manresa starts. God begins to make his presence felt, with elemental, pictorial representations, acting with him "as a schoolteacher deals with a child." These representations have to do with subjects that will be dominant, all the rest of his life: the creation of the world, the Eucharist, the humanity of Christ, and, in the shape of very concrete images, the Trinity. The earlier mentions of saints in his Autobiography now disappear. In their place, he bursts into a surprising paragraph about "his great devotion to the Most Holy Trinity," which is becoming a dominant theme in his spiritual life, to the point that "he could not stop talking about the Most Holy Trinity, with many different comparisons and great joy and consolation."

Ignatius has survived the testing of penances and desolation, and this third phase of his stay at Manresa reveals a greater maturity and serenity and an apostolic thrust. "After God began to comfort him, seeing the fruit he was obtaining when dealing with souls," he gave up those extremes he had formerly observed, and he now cut his nails and his hair." So far, he has done what lay in his power: an unreserved surrender, a merciless purification, a spiritually discerned acceptance of God's lights, an availability for apostolic conversations and activity. It was, humanly speaking, all that was needed to ready him for the definitive sign. And it was not long coming.

— "The Trinitarian Inspiration
of the Ignatian Charism" in *SL* 89–91

The Cardoner River

It was in August or September of 1522, barely fifteen months after he is wounded at Pamplona and seven after his coming to Manresa. In that brief time he has gone through a very long spiritual journey. He goes out of Manresa one day to make a devotional visit to an outlying church. The road follows the edge of a steep hillside, at the foot of which flows the Cardoner.

> As he went along occupied with his devotions, he sat down for a little while with his face toward the river the eyes of his understanding began to be opened. Not that he saw any vision; rather, understanding and knowing many things, both spiritual things and matters of faith and learning, with so intense an enlightenment that everything seemed new to him. Though there were many, he cannot set forth the details that he understood then, except that he experienced a great clarity in his understanding. So much so that in the whole course of his life, through sixty-two years, even if he gathered up all the many helps he has had from God and all the many things he has learned and "added them together," he does not think they would amount to as much as he received on that one occasion. After this had lasted for a good while, he went to kneel before a nearby cross to give thanks to God. (*The Autobiography of St. Ignatius*)

Ignatius's mention of "that so great illumination" is extremely significant. It has been for him a sort of Pentecost that marks an end of his past and lights the light of a different future. When he dictates his autobiography in 1555, the year before his death, the effulgence of that mystical experience, of a loftiness that his Diary reveals to us, is still shining brilliantly in his memory. I believe that there are three angles from which we can view that enlightenment:

First, the nature of the grace received. Let us remember that the words Ignatius uses are not casual. He is at the end of his life, when his sense of exactitude has grown very strong and his mystical encounters have left him with unparalleled experience. After his initial mention of "that so great illumination," Ignatius puts great emphasis on a distinction: "not that he saw...; rather, understanding and knowing." That is to say, there is a radical, qualitative change with regard to his earlier illuminations, which were only in his imagination and apt only for rudimentary manifestations. These are now "intellectual lights, directly infused by God into his intelligence. At Manresa, Ignatius moves into the highest infused contemplation." He also stresses a quantitative aspect, saying that he received more help and knowledge on that occasion than in all the rest of his life. That may have been an overstatement, though hyperbole was not a habitual defect in Ignatius. But even if it were an overstatement, the fact of falling into it here would not be without significance.

Second, the content of the illumination. The terms that Ignatius used are very exact, but very generic too. Polanco says that "Father Ignatius explained in detail to no one the secret of this vision, since it was so hard to communicate his experiences. But he did mention the fact to them." And he had good reason to do so. The enlightenment of the Cardoner is the most influential spiritual fact in Ignatius's life previous to La Storta, and that gives it a transcendental importance in that prefoundation period up till 1538, when he was gathering his friends from Paris and mulling over the germinal ideas of the Society. While he was winning them over, one by one, "they were resolute in following Father Ignatius and his way of proceeding." In those long years of intimacy and confidences, Ignatius no doubt informed them about what had happened by the Cardoner — without going into details, as Polanco notes, but still telling them in general what it had meant. . . .

In any event, if we consider the enlightenment of the Cardoner as the extraordinary climax in a series of such illuminations that really had started and built up in preceding weeks, we can describe its content more or less this way: it is an infused intellectual illumination about the divine essence and the Trinity of Persons in a generic way and, more concretely, about two of its outwardly directed operations: the creation and the incarnation. Ignatius is brought into the *trinitarian* intimacy and finds himself an illumined spectator of the creation and incarnation in a trinitarian context. "The descent of creatures from God and their necessary re-ascent and reintegration into their ultimate end, God himself, is one of the most vivid experiences of the great enlightenment." Ignatius is, without realizing it, in an eminently Pauline theological line. This trinitarian context will be clearly detectable in the *Exercises*. Not only in Ignatius's presentation of the mystery of the incarnation, but in the "Principle and Foundation," too, which he will write later, if we judge by the philosophical elements in it, which the pilgrim at Manresa was not yet educated enough to compose.

Third, the meaning and consequences of the illumination. Manresa was for Ignatius what Damascus was for St. Paul and the burning bush for Moses: a mysterious theophany that inaugurates and synthesizes his mission, a call to set out on an obscure road that will keep opening up before him as he follows it. On the spot, Ignatius is transformed. Laínez writes a marginal note in Câmara's Autobiography: "And this left him with his understanding so profoundly enlightened that it seemed to him he was a different man and had a different intellect than he had before."

The *transformation* of Ignatius is manifest. The least important change is that now he makes himself presentable and becomes more sociable, softens down his harshness and takes on a more ordered, human rhythm of life. Chiefly, it is his inner self that changes: his spirituality, until then individualist and introspective, is turned completely around, becoming more and more communitary and apostolic. His pilgrimage to Jerusalem loses its penitential motivation and becomes a meeting with Christ in the places where he lived and died, and where Ignatius will want to stay to continue the Lord's work.

The greatest transformation, though, is that he finds a methodology for all his further progress, the supreme lesson with which the Lord, who had been guiding him like a child, culminates the Manresa period of his schooling. Let us state this in Nadal's words: "There he learned to discern spirits." Polanco, who follows Laínez's line of testimony, says the same thing: "That light (received at the Cardoner) had to do concretely with distinguishing good and evil spirits." That *knowledge* is all the more necessary — and will be so in the future too, for him and for the Society — as he still perceives his apostolic vocation in only an extremely vague way and he will constantly need some technique for clarifying it.

— "The Trinitarian Inspiration
of the Ignatian Charism" in *SL* 91–96

La Storta

La Storta is a place ten miles from Rome, where a small chapel stands at the intersection of the ancient Roman Road along which they were coming and a lateral road. Ignatius, with Diego Laínez and Pierre Favre, entered the village "and making a prayer, felt such a change coming over his soul and saw so clearly that God the Father was placing him with Christ his Son that he could not doubt that God the Father was indeed placing him with his Son." This is the sum total of what we know about the event that Ignatius will recount eighteen years later.

But Laínez, who was present and no doubt received immediate and detailed confidences, has spelled out for us the content of that illumination, which could not have more far-reaching consequences. And Ignatius has stated that "all that Laínez said was true." What Laínez said and later wrote was this: Ignatius was singularly favored by spiritual feelings all during the trip from Vicenza to La Storta, especially when he would receive communion from the hand of Favre or Laínez himself. He had the sensation at La Storta that the Father was impressing these words on his heart: I will be propitious to you in Rome. On the occasion we are referring to, Ignatius felt he could "see Christ with his cross on his shoulder and together with him the Father, who was telling him: I want you to serve us. For this reason, Ignatius, taking great devotion from that most holy name, wanted the congregation to be called the Society of Jesus" (Laínez).

The profound meaning of this enlightenment is very clear: the Divine Persons accept him into their service. It is the divine confirmation that Ignatius wanted at that crucial moment of his life. The generic call of the Cardoner is now explicitly and formally restated. Just as had happened at the time of "that so great illumination," the habitual low-key Ignatian prose style bursts into flame: "he felt such a change coming over his soul and saw so vividly." . . .

The Person who dominates the scene is the Father, not the Son. It is the Father who accepts Ignatius and gives him to the Son, just as it is the Father who promises to be propitious to them in Rome. Ignatius, creator of this apostolic group and bearer of the virtual charism of the Society whose existence is assured at that very moment, is received as the servant of Jesus, and of the Father in Jesus. He has attained the grace that is asked for in the colloquy of the Two Standards: "to be received under his standard" into complete poverty and humility, which is the meaning of the Son's appearing to him, not in his infancy or preaching or resurrection, but carrying his cross. There is also the same Ignatian line of intercessors: through Mary to her Son, through the Son to the Father. The christology underlying these illuminations fits into the purest Pauline and Johannine tradition of leading everything back to the Father.

With such enlightenments from the Divine Persons, Ignatius is as if led by the hand toward what the Society will be. No one has synthesized better than Nadal the meaning of that pre-foundational period. He writes, "Ignatius was following the spirit, he was not running ahead of it. And yet he was being led gently, whither he did not know. He was not intending at that time to found the order. Little by little, though, the road was opening up before him and he was moving along it, wisely ignorant, with his heart placed very simply in Christ." The complete promise of the future Society is given in those lines.

•

Ignatius was apparently unable to settle for anything less. Such, in any event, is his tendency to carry things to the very ultimate. The former gentleman at court and captain on the battlefield always spurned mediocrity and compromises, he aspired for the noblest lady, he wanted to outstrip the saints, later he would refuse to leave a court trial without getting a verdict. "Our Father Ignatius had a great character, a great soul, and with the further help of our Lord's grace he always strove to undertake great things" (Nadal). He will be the one who pursues the *magis*, the greater glory of God. Kneeling before the Trinity, that fontal mystery of the divine essence, Ignatius follows his wildest ambitions and accepts his own "measure" — the mystery of how his puniness and unworthiness are called to collaborate in the divine action.

— "The Trinitarian Inspiration
of the Ignatian Charism" in *SL* 105–7, 110

Ignatius in Rome

Natural calamities and disasters — like outbreaks of famine, epidemics, catastrophes — make demands on our charity for assistance and help that can brook no delay. The practical conduct of Ignatius in this matter is of a decisively instructive value for us. His action as General is the irreplaceable "practical implementation" of the *Constitutions* that we must make our own. Ignatius teaches us by his deeds the primacy that charity — even initiatives of material assistance — can and must have, in given circumstances, in the totality of the Society's apostolic activity.

The Famine Stricken

The winter of 1538 — the second winter for the first companions in Rome — has gone down in history as "the winter of famine." People were living in a situation of emergency. The harvest had all but failed. Ignatius's own problems were gigantic. The campaign of defamation let loose by his slanderers threatened to ruin his whole work of founding the Society, so that he had to spend entire days in the official lobbies and the courts until he obtained a sentence of acquittal on November 18. He had yet another problem to face. Precisely at this time there elapsed the year of waiting to which Ignatius and his companions had bound themselves by the vow of making a pilgrimage to Jerusalem, with the result that they were all deeply taken up with concern for their future. It is during this week, running from November 18 to 23, that they take the decisive step of presenting themselves to Pope Paul III. As if all this were not enough, Ignatius was busy, on a personal level, with a matter of the greatest importance, the celebration of his First Mass, since the reason for its delay had disappeared with the cancellation of the voyage to Jerusalem. Can we really imagine the spiritual earnestness with which Ignatius prepared himself for this fresh encounter with Christ? These, then, were the circumstances in which he and his nine companions gave themselves totally to the assistance of the famine-stricken of Rome. So intense and profound was this experience that all the early historical sources of the Society dwell on its details when reporting it. Ignatius and his companions would set out at early dawn from their new residence — the house of Antonio Frangipani, next to the Tower of Melangolo — to beg for bread, wood, and straw to lie on; then they would carry it all on their shoulders to their poor apartments. Going out again, they would gather the beggars and starving people, who literally lay in the slush of the streets of Rome, bring them together, and make them comfortable as best they could — some four hundred of them at a time — or offer them some ration of food. Thus they were able to help more than three thousand persons in a city which then counted scarcely forty thousand inhabitants.

Aid to the Oppressed and Exploited Groups

Ignatius is not satisfied with a charity that offers material assistance merely on an individual basis. His inner vision leads him to discover the collective, sad plight of very definite social groups. His charity drives him to make every effort to obtain for them a more just treatment at the hands of social structures....

Beggars. Begging had been banned in Rome. There as in other places, then as now, it was a social scourge in which authentic need got mixed up with shrewd swindling. But an indiscriminate ban had succeeded in further aggravating the sorry plight of the truly poor of those days, when there was no social security, unemployment subsidy, or old-age pension. The poor and the sick, the old and the crippled filled the streets of Rome. Ignatius assisted those that he could. For all, he obtained from the pope a decree which mitigated the ban and established the "Society of Orphans," which was to be charged with the task of sifting "the poor who were sick or crippled in any way" from those "able-bodied" others that were capable of doing work.

Prostitutes. Prostitutes represented a class that was at once exploited, maintained, and despised by a hypocritical society. To them, too, Ignatius directs his charity, to free them as a group from the unjust structure that oppressed them. There were already other institutions that were helping them. But it was unjust that such institutions accepted only those who agreed to spend the rest of their lives as penitents in a religious order. Ignatius rejected this as making it difficult and painful for these women to change their lives. He contended that this was in effect coercion, against the freedom of the person. He founded his own work, "The House of St. Martha," to which he admitted not only those who wished to enter religion as penitents, but also others, married women and spinsters, particularly those who were known in Rome as "reputable courtesans," frequented by the nobility. All these were helped by Ignatius until some definitive solution was found for them: either rejoining their husbands, or marriage for the spinsters, or religious life, or some decent position. "A charming sight" — writes Pedro de Ribadeneira — "to see this holy old man walking ahead of one of those unfortunate women, still young and good-looking, making way, as it were, and opening a path for her." In keeping with his way of doing things, Ignatius also established a lay association, "The Society of Grace," to see that the work of St. Martha was carried on.... From his own poor resources Ignatius drew money to finance the new institution, but at what great cost and with what trouble! His house of

Santa Maria della Strada was full to overflowing with Jesuits, and money was scarce. And yet, when his administrator Pietro Codacio discovered huge blocks of stone and marble, remains of Roman monuments, in a wooded clearing that belonged to the Jesuits, Ignatius had yet another burst and impulse of charity. "Sell those stones that you have removed, and from them obtain for me a sum amounting to one hundred ducats." That considerable amount was all for the house of St. Martha — and this, let us never forget, in the financial circumstances in which Ignatius was!"

Young women in danger. Scarcely had he handed over to others the work of St. Martha, when Ignatius, in his characteristic way, embarked on another, "The Association of Downtrodden Young Women," a work of prevention, of social protection of women, we might say today. Ignatius encouraged wealthy and charitable persons to enroll in it and obtained pontifical approval for it. Similarly he established a group of twelve trustworthy citizens through whose good offices he distributed help to those ashamed to identify themselves as poor. With it was born "The Society of the Most Blessed Sacrament," under the supervision of the General of the Society of Jesus.

I ask myself what would have been Ignatius's attitude today in the face of the calamities of our times: the boat-people, the starving thousands in the Sahara belt, the refugees and forced migrants of today. What would have been his attitude in the face of the suffering of such clearly defined groups of victims of criminal exploitation, as are, for example, the drug addicts? Would we be mistaken in thinking that Ignatius, in our times, would have done more than we are doing, that he would have acted in a way different from us?

Ignatius had arrived at this intelligent practice of charity by two routes: by the roads of personal experience and by that of spiritual choice. Ignatius had been poor, voluntarily poor, painfully poor, a real beggar. He had learned to value charity in his own personal experience of need. He walked the streets of Manresa, Barcelona, Alcalá, Salamanca, and Paris; he wandered through the ports of Barcelona, Haifa, and Gaeta; he traversed the routes of Flanders and England, begging only to eat poorly. He gave up the remnants of his alms when he felt the need to surrender more completely into the provident hands of God. If at times during his studies he kept the donations given him, it was out of a firm conviction of an "ordered and discerning love" directed toward himself. But, already in 1536, he wrote that his desire was to remain always in such a condition as "to preach as a poor man, and certainly not with the embarrassing abundance I now enjoy by reason of my studies. However that may be, as a pledge of what I here say, I am going to send you, when my studies are finished, the few books I now have, or may have then." Ignatius had experienced the value of the charity of others in his own poverty. When General of the Society, he poured out his own love and charity most generously onto the poverty of others.

It is not at all surprising, therefore, that charity is a constant point of reference in Ignatius's spiritual teaching. I shall say nothing here of charity as a spiritual option, such as it is presented in the *Exercises* or institutionalized in the *Constitutions*. But I must refer, even if only in passing, to the place occupied by charity in Ignatius's letters. In the letters addressed to his relatives in Loyola or to his benefactors in Barcelona, to his protectors or simply to those whom he directed spiritually — persons of great rank or of lowly condition — to the Jesuits scattered over Europe or Asia, in all these letters a prominent place is repeatedly given to almsgiving, visits to hospitals and prisons, assistance to those in need. This type of recommendation is, of course, never missing in the instructions with which

Ignatius sends someone on a "mission" — be that to Trent, Germany, England, or Sicily — or for the founding of houses or of colleges. Indeed, it would seem that for Ignatius no ministry or service, be it ever so spiritual in itself, could be deemed complete were it not complemented by the charitable works of material assistance, and vice versa. For it is clear that, for Ignatius, the true exercise of love for one's fellow human beings is apostolic zeal, the ardent desire to procure their salvation and perfection. But it is no less evident that Ignatius loves people whole and entire, as did the Lord for whose sake alone he loves.

— "Rooted and Grounded in Love"
in *SL* 165–71

THE SPIRITUAL EXERCISES OF IGNATIUS

During his time at Manresa in 1522–23, Ignatius began keeping track of his spiritual experiences, reflecting on them and writing them down in a notebook. In the years after his conversion, especially when he came to Paris, he would lead others through a variety of meditations and contemplations based on what he had learned from his own experience. His aim was to awaken in them the quality of spiritual ardor that had come alive in him. This was the origin of his "Spiritual Exercises." This process draws the believer into a vivid encounter with the Jesus of the Gospels. Divided into four parts, or "Weeks," that focus in turn on the themes of conversion from sin, the call to discipleship, the passion of Jesus, and the resurrection of Jesus, the aim of the Exercises, in the words of St. Ignatius, is "to overcome oneself and to order one's life, without reaching a decision through some disordered affection." Hence, the spiritual program of Ignatius is geared toward genuine freedom. It opens one's eyes to the deep truth of reality and equips one with the tools for discerning how one is called to follow Christ. In all this, the aim is to help one become more fully united to God. The Exercises thus integrates three classical dimensions of Christian mysticism — the purgative, illuminative, and unitive ways.

As a text, the Spiritual Exercises *functions as an "exercise" manual. It is not a book that someone takes up to "read" but to "use" as a guide for one's spiritual practice. In fact, the text of the* Exercises *is less for the retreatant than the director. From the earliest days of the Society of Jesus, Ignatius and his companions used the Exercises to initiate new members into their distinctive form of religious life. At the same time, they drew on them for their own spiritual nourishment throughout the rest of their lives. Hence, Jesuits developed the practice of engaging in a shorter version of the Exercises every year and making the full thirty-day retreat not only during novitiate, but later during the time of preparation for final vows called tertianship. Indeed, the practice of undertaking the Exercises and directing others in them spread far beyond the Society of Jesus. Many religious orders of women and men integrate the Exercises of Ignatius into their own spiritualities, and countless lay men and women have found in the Exercises a powerful aid for living a genuine mysticism in the world.*

The Spiritual Exercises *of St. Ignatius stands as a classic text of Christian spirituality. Its appearance marks a massive paradigm shift in the history of Christianity, just as the founding of the Society of Jesus initiates a new era in the history of religious life. Pedro Arrupe grasped all this. He understood both the historical importance of the Exercises, and their immediate relevance in the ongoing life of the church. He perceived that if the Society of Jesus were to respond wholeheartedly to the call for renewal issued by Vatican II, it would need above all to revitalize its own practice of making and giving the Spiritual*

Exercises. That this renewal took place with such impressive energy, creativity, and fidelity must be counted as one of the great accomplishments of the postconciliar Society led by Arrupe.

*The three sets of selections gathered in this section betray a range of genres, tones, and settings. The first selection, **The Exercises and the Society of Jesus,** recalls the crucial link between the Jesuit charism and the Spiritual Exercises while noting that, in a real sense, the Exercises "belong to" the entire church. The second, **Addressing the World of Today,** is a brief quotation taken from Arrupe's book-length interview with Jean-Claude Dietsch. Its personal and passionate tone complements its expansive scope. The third set of selections, **Following the Pattern of Scripture,** indicates how the dynamic of the Exercises flows from the pedagogy of love in the Old Testament, and the devotion to Christ and his mission as told in the New Testament.*

The Exercises and the Society of Jesus

We all know well how the consciousness of the vocation to the Society was awakened in each one of us. We know also that the Society itself originated historically in the same way. The decisive element of our own particular charism resulted from an access to the light of the Gospel and to the Person of Jesus Christ, afforded us by the Spiritual Exercises of St. Ignatius.

In the Exercises St. Ignatius foresaw his future dedication to the church and to the neighbor. From the Exercises sprang forth the group which one day was to offer itself to Paul III "desiring to be called Company of Jesus" and asking "to be sent to any part of the world where there was hope of greater service of God and greater help for the neighbor." From the Exercises have come forth, one by one, all the Jesuits, from the beginning until today. This is what marks them and constitutes them, before any law or constitution. The *Constitutions* and the rules are to be understood always as the concrete application of the spirit of the Exercises to the exigencies of an apostolic order, flexible and available for the service of the church of the human family.

The Exercises are not a stereotyped mold, a machine to fashion wholesale persons completely uniform, with subdued personalities. They constitute a simple method of prayer, of meditation and contemplation of the life of Jesus Christ, of examination to know oneself and conquer oneself, "to order one's life without being affected by any inordinate attachment." They are a spiritual experience, which ought to be personal, though under direction, and allow oneself to be guided by the Spirit, learning to discern him; tarrying where one meets him "without being anxious to go further." It is not strange, then, if within the common inspiration, the Exercises engender, in each of those who make them and in each epoch of their application, a diversity of orientations and of concrete determinations in the Christian and apostolic life. Just as personal experience, the experience of the Exercises is historical in character, always old and always new, ever the same and changing with the circumstances.

In reality, this variety stems from the infinite efficacy of the Gospel, to which the Exercises give access. The Exercises have, certainly, their own special manner of access to the Gospel. They suppose on the part of the one making them the personal decision, the generous commitment of himself or herself even to the "folly" of the third degree of humility, the reflection and maturity, the apostolic dynamism of love. They lay stress on the humanity of Jesus Christ, on the appeal to the love of friendship and to following him closely, on the enterprise of the Kingdom.

But all these particular features have not limited much the spectrum of possibilities opened up by the Exercises. In fact, though holding the Exercises as a family treasure, the Jesuits have not guarded it jealously; they have understood that it was a common good, and they have offered it to the church. And much of recent spirituality has been fostered by the Exercises.

— "The Jesuit and the Christ of the Spiritual Exercises" in *OA* 256–58

Addressing the World of Today

I believe that the Spiritual Exercises have an extraordinary timeliness, through what they offer and through their impact toward changing the heart of a person. That is precisely what the world of today needs. The terrible human problems which agonize our contemporaries will not find solutions in laws or in reforms of structures unless the human hearts change beforehand. As a matter of fact, it is people who create the structures and the various economic systems. Consequently, if people do not change interiorly, the new structures and new financial systems will be as bad, or worse, than the preceding ones. For this reason, the Exercises, which aim precisely at personal conversion and reform of one's life in accordance with the Gospel, possess a peculiar strength for the building of a new world — a new world which would mean an integral and genuine human progress, and not a world in which humankind is a prisoner and victim of its own selfishness or of its inventions. It is against itself that a technocratic and egoistical humanity transforms the world into a prison and builds what is called the "city of mammon" in which there remains only, according to somebody's words, "the wind passing through." It has also been said that "a sound renovation springs from all the potentialities of humankind." The Exercises have this power of provoking a total response to the

call of Christ from a person facing life's choices. The Exercises
inspire true evaluation and true discernment of concrete human
problems. And they display their greatest efficacy in action, with
solutions which will be the best because they will be born of
a balanced spirit which does not come under influences which
could disturb it.

— *"The Society as an Apostolic Body"* in *OJ* 67

Following the Pattern of Scripture

It is interesting to note that the "pedagogy of love in the Exercises" seems to follow the exact lines of the pedagogy of love in
Old Testament revelation. It is not a theory of love that is pro-
pounded, but an experiential pedagogy that is practiced. Love
is presented as the constant agent of all that leads to salvation:
from creation ... to the barricade set up between humanity and
hell, even unto the plan of redemption, the call to reciprocal
love and to the service of cooperation. One might say that Ignatius puts his retreatant under a sort of irresistible pressure of
proofs of the love of God, a love that is made manifest more
in deeds than in words through repeated acts of self-giving that
culminate in the surrender and gift of his only Son. In this way,
Ignatius means to set in motion a process of complete transformation in retreatants: the purification of their heart and the
right ordering of their affective faculty. In a word, his objective
is to get the retreatants to live the truth of God's own love and
their love for God by giving themselves in service.

— "Rooted and Grounded in Love"
in *SL* 147–48

•

The Exercises are, in the last analysis, a method in the pedagogy of love — the pedagogy, that is, of the most pure charity

toward God and toward one's neighbor. They root out carnal and worldly love from the human heart, thus opening it to the beams of God's love. A demanding love it is, calling forth in a person a response of love and of service. Service, which is itself love. This is the message of the very last paragraph of the book of the *Exercises*. "The zealous service of God our Lord out of pure love should be esteemed above all." In the Exercises we find terms and concepts which are logically reducible to one another: the "glory of God," for example, can be replaced by the "service of God." The same may be said of "praise" and "reverence." Only one term is final and irreducible to any other: love.

— "Rooted and Grounded in Love"

in *SL* 152

•

For Ignatius the key to the Gospel is to be found in the person of Christ and in his condition as that of being one "sent" from the Father in mission to humanity, and this implies the incarnation — his identification of the human with himself — and his death for humanity. The whole of the Exercises revolves around the person of "the Lord who has become human for me." The life of Christ, especially his public life, his passion, and his resurrection, are a living reality which the retreatant ought to meditate upon "as though I were present there," asking with insistence for "an intimate knowledge of our Lord... that I may love and follow him better." Christ appears to the eyes of the retreatant as the Eternal King to whom is present the whole world; and to the world, and to each person, he gives the same invitation to work for all others, "and thus to enter into the glory of my Father." For the retreatant, Christ chooses so many persons, apostles, disciples, etc., and sends them throughout the world to spread his sacred doctrines.

The Christ of the Gospel is seen and experienced in the Exercises as Christ who is poor, humble, the servant who is obedient to the Father; as the Christ of the *kenosis,* "taking the form of a slave" (Phil. 2:7) who has become one of "the many," like one needing redemption. He is the Christ of the Beatitudes and the Christ of the cross. When he sends his disciples to continue his mission, he sends them as neighbors to people, as unconditional servants of all people in fulfillment of the will of the Father. He sends them in poverty, to be humiliated as he was and, like him, to suffer and be laden with injuries for the redemption of the world.   — "The Exercises and the Jesuit" in *OA* 278

•

In the Exercises, we contemplate the person of Christ in action, in the mysteries of his mortal life, and we use our senses to grasp him. "Look in imagination, meditating and studying in detail his situation." "Listen to what he is saying or might say." The retreatant "should imagine that he is watching Christ our Lord taking a meal with his disciples; he should study his manner of eating and drinking, looking and talking." He should conduct himself "as a poor servant, looking after all their wants. See, observe, and study what they are saying. See and reflect on what they are doing: the journey they have to make, the hardships they have to put up with." . . .

Ignatius feels powerfully drawn toward Christ and sees him as the justification and model for his work. With an ironclad logic, he himself takes the triple step that he recommends in the Exercises: to know Christ, love him, follow him. In great things as in small things, Ignatius is ever constant in that love which, at his conversion, makes him want to know — at the cost of dangers and penalties not easily imaginable today — whatever remains on this earth that is connected with and evocative of the person of Christ: the holy places. His own way of proceeding, and the way of proceeding he wants for his Society, in great things as in small, is this: to imitate perfectly Christ, who was perfectly God, but also perfectly human.

— "Our Way of Proceeding" in *SL* 58, 59

•

In the Spiritual Exercises we see that the motive force of our lives is to be found in the personal love for Christ. This personal love of Christ expresses itself in a total commitment "under the standard of the cross," where one chooses poverty and suffering and humiliation rather than riches and glory. The evangelical attitude of the third degree of humility that is expected of every Jesuit coincides with the attitude portrayed in the third class of human beings. Compromise has no place here, and the Jesuit must, with a tremendous detachment, be open to the Spirit, always looking for God's will and God's greater glory. This epitomizes our spirituality, and this is what the Society of Jesus has to give to the world.

— "Relevance of the Society and Its Apostolate
in the World of Today" in *OA* 17

THE IGNATIAN MYSTICISM OF LOVE

Arrupe's last major theological essay on Ignatian spirituality touches on its most profound root: the power of love. Appropriately entitled "Rooted and Grounded in Love," this exhortation, although addressed specifically to the worldwide Society of Jesus, belongs to everyone who has been moved by the spirituality of Ignatius. In it Arrupe reflects on the Christian intuition that links love of God with love of neighbor, an intuition utterly central to Ignatius's contemplation in action.

*The three selections here come from "Rooted and Grounded in Love." The brief selection that introduces this section, **The Power of Love**, opens the essay and announces its central message. In the second selection, Arrupe meditates on the mysticism of love as it appears in the Gospel of John and the letters of Paul, revealing at the same time the biblical roots of Ignatius's and his own "mysticism of love." In the final selection, **The Apocalyptic Finality of Love**, he draws on Matthew's Gospel to speak forcefully about the dialectic between love (agape) and wickedness (anomia). Here we see one of the most telling aspects of Arrupe's "mysticism of open eyes" (see Introduction, p. 31). Arrupe does not seek a conceptual "solution" to the problem of suffering (theodicy), but draws our gaze back to the power of love: the divine power of "a disinterested impulse that leads us to understand, to empathize, to share, to help, and to heal."*

The Power of Love

"Love is the weighty power of the soul." This is what Ignatius wrote to a former companion and fellow student of his Paris days, without knowing perhaps that he was quoting St. Augustine. And certainly, without intending to do so, he was bequeathing to us the most incisive formulation possible of his own spiritual journey, and of the charism of the Society.

— "Rooted and Grounded in Love"
in *SL* 146

Love in St. Paul and St. John

Ignatius had succeeded in perfectly unifying his love of God, a "most intense love directed totally to loving the Most Holy Trinity," with love for other people. This is the model of charity that the *Exercises* and the *Constitutions* ask of us, the integration of charity that Paul, the apostle of service to the neighbor, and John, the apostle of love of God, proclaimed and lived.

Paul, like Ignatius, was a convert, passionately dedicated to Christ, to whom he showed his love by an intense service in the defense and spread of the faith. Very few are the times, though, when he mentions that love explicitly in his letters. He uses other expressions instead: living for Christ, walking toward Christ, anathema on anyone who does not love Christ, and the like. Yet his love impelled him to serve his brothers and sisters, whom he loved as intensely as he loved Christ. This tension becomes evident in one of his most beautiful texts. "I am caught in this dilemma: I want to be gone and be with Christ, which would be very much the better, but for me to stay alive in this body is a more urgent need for your sake" (Phil. 1:23). Paul is sure that he will continue to live with them. For if as he tells the Corinthians, he feels the overwhelming drive of the love of Christ, it is precisely because he realizes that Christ has died for all, "so that the living should live no longer for themselves, but for him who died and was raised to life for them" (2 Cor. 5:14). Moreover, his love for Christ contains an apostolic thrust, and thus the best way Paul knows to satisfy his thirst for identification with Christ is by devoting himself to the service of others, concretely of the "gentiles." This service is owed to all, inasmuch as in every person, notably in the weaker ones, there is a brother or sister for whom Christ died" (1 Cor. 8:11).

John's teaching is identical, but in a more explicitly trinitarian framework, because for him the relationship among the Father, the Word, and human beings is more explicit. "God loved the world so much that he gave his only Son, so that everyone who believes in him may not be lost but may have eternal life" (John 3:16). This insertion of human beings into

the heart of divine love takes place radically in the very bo-
som of the Trinity. "The Father loves me because I lay down
my life" (John 10:17), and "the Father himself loves you for
loving me" (John 16:27). John keeps coming back to this idea.
"Anybody who loves me will be loved by my Father" (John
14:21). He comes to it from many different angles. "As the
Father has loved me, so I have loved you" (John 15:9). Moreover, this same John who so clearly states the love relationship
among the Father, the Son, and every human being adds to it
our charity — love for our brothers and sisters — which is the
commandment that Jesus calls "mine" and "new." Christ, who
set the commandment of love for our brothers and sisters alongside the first commandment of loving God, seems to invert the
terms. We must love our brothers and sisters so that we can
say that we love God. We love our neighbor, not only as Christ
loved us, but because Christ loved us. And it is by loving our
neighbor that we love Christ and the Father. John explains this
in the words of Jesus. He leaves the world, but yet remains in
each one of us. Hence we must remain united, since his presence links us together. We must be "one" as he and the Father
are one. This union through love will be the witness by which
the world will come to believe that the Son has been sent. . . .

In the first of his letters John dwells on the inseparableness of
love of God from love of neighbor, understanding love-charity
in its operative aspect as gift of self and sharing. The theological root — the "root and foundation" in Paul's metaphor — is
the very divine essence. "God is love." So absolutely is he love
that "love comes from God and . . . anyone who fails to love can
never have known God" (1 John 4:7–8). A love that consists
in the giving of self, the supreme evidence of which was given
when the Father sent "his Son to be the sacrifice that takes our
sins away." Immediately John draws the consequences of this.

"Since God has loved us so much, we too should love one another." And then his final conclusion: "As long as we love one another God will live in us and his love will be complete in us" (1 John 4:10–12). God the Father wanted it this way because so it had to be. Neither the love that is in him, nor the love that he has put into us, can be broken up into separate parts. It is a drive that is total and indivisible in us just as it is one in God. We love God because he gave us his Son. We love our brothers and sisters because the Son gave himself for them and is in them. Responding to the Father's love with our love for our brothers and sisters, we share in the divine life that is love.

This communion of mutual love in Christ among brothers and sisters is community — *koinonia* — that shared attitude of service for one's brothers and sisters that shows itself in deeds. In the Society of Jesus, this *koinonia* issuing from fraternal love constitutes the totality of our mission to help others to "believe" — in the Johannine sense of a proclamation of the faith and a dedication to Christ — by spreading the faith and by helping them to love one another by promoting justice among them. Love for our sisters and brothers is an expression of our being children of God. "Whoever loves the Father that begot him loves the child whom be begets. We can be sure that we love God's children if we love God himself and do what he has commanded us" (1 John 5:1). We cannot love God cut off from others, nor in the abstract. It is a trilateral love. To love our brothers and sisters, and to show this love in our actions, is not something adventitious, something added to our love of God to complete it. It is a constitutive element demanded by the very notion of the love of God.

But we must make the converse statement, too. By the very fact that we are Christians, we cannot genuinely love others unless we love God. What is asked of us is not an abstract love of humanity ("philanthropy") but a concrete love of brothers

and sisters ("philadelphia"). In every person, with all his or her concrete circumstances, there is a value that does not depend on me, but that makes that person like me. God is within the other, with his love, waiting for me. And this is a call that I cannot neglect. To refuse love — and the service that goes with love — even to a single person is to refuse to recognize that person's dignity and, at the same time, to abdicate my own, which has no better foundation than the dignity of the other. It is most important to keep clearly in mind this equality of dignity between each of us and other people, if we are to grasp the viciousness there is in hatred, in the abuse of the freedom of others, in exploitation, in a word, in the lack of mercy. *Anomia* — contempt for and generalized violation of law, the predominance of selfishness — has its clearest condemnation in *agape,* that disinterested and active love which should reign among human beings. In the unavoidable clash of interests at the heart of our complex human relations, only the values that unify us all can resolve the conflict. We have to accept that even the most solidly founded rights of some must at times yield to the needs of others. God receives in others the love we have for him, and he accepts and cherishes as a service the sacrifice of what we have been given as his children, but yield in the name of brotherhood. The presence of each person in my life becomes, transcendentally, a form of the presence of God, and my acceptance of my brothers and sisters becomes my implicit acceptance of God. This is what Juan Alfaro has called the "sacrament of our neighbor."   — "Rooted and Grounded in Love"
in *SL* 171–74

The Apocalyptic Finality of Love

Yes, justice is not enough. The world needs a stronger cure, a more effective witness, and more effective deeds: those of love.

When we glance over the newspaper headlines and seek somehow for the real reason why human relations are at such a low ebb — within the family, the state, the world of work, the economic order, and internationally — every explanation in terms of justice and injustice seems inadequate. Never have people talked so much about justice, and yet never has justice been so flagrantly disregarded. This reminds me of the scene with which Matthew begins the apocalyptic section of his Gospel. It is a short literary sketch, drawn with strong and expressive strokes. It contains one verse that is worth its weight in gold, a deep, stark, and accurate explanation of what is happening today: "Such will be the spread of wickedness that love in most people will grow cold" (Matt. 24:12). Wickedness and love are expressed in the original Greek by the two words: *anomia* and *agape*. The two grow in inverse proportion one to the other. It is important to dwell a while on these two concepts.

Anomia is, as many versions translate it, wickedness. Literally, it is the total absence of law, or the violation and scorn of law. It is the exaltation of selfishness with no regard at all for the norm, the flouting of law; in a word, injustice. It is the repetition of that primeval pride which led to humanity's fall — the first sin — and which keeps sin in the world even today. In the Gospel text just quoted, *anomia* is related to the chaos described in the preceding lines: wars, famines, calamities, false rumors. Human beings, who are at once promoters and victims of this *anomia*, compound the evils: false redeemers, treachery, desertion, widespread hatred. These are the disastrous consequences of the disregard for justice, of the protection of one's own interests to the detriment of others' rights and needs, and the detriment of the common good. The right of might replaces the might of right: it nullifies God's command, revealed in Jesus, that love and solidarity should rule the relationships among human beings. It is, in the technical sense, the rule of

immorality, ethical degeneration. *Anomia* is the absence of justice, iniquity in its etymological sense: the absence of equity,
injustice.

Agape (a favorite word with John, but one that in Matthew
appears only in this text) is disinterested love, the urge to self-
giving that our benevolence toward others prompts us to. It
is the word that aptly expresses God's love for us. It is the
sort of love among human beings that Christ termed his commandment, the new commandment. It is the sign that we have
"known" the Father. For those who do not believe, it is the
guarantee and test of the faith that is alive in us. *Agape*-love, in
contradistinction to *eros,* is the center around which history is
unified, just as *anomia* is history's divisive factor. Because, we
must remember, although *agape* is the term for both our love of
God and our love for one another, we are using it here in the
second sense. This is clear by the fact that it is contrasted with
anomia, and evident from the content of this entire eschatological section of Matthew, which ends precisely by exalting love
and charity toward our brothers and sisters as the criterion of
sifting at the Last Judgment (Matt. 25:31–46).

Agape and *anomia* are antithetical. Matthew centers the
cosmic distress of the final age on this duel between *anomia*-
wickedness-injustice and *agape*-love. *Anomia:* we seem to be
reading the chronicle of contemporary history. An assault on
humanity, an arbitrary and violent imposition of authority over
persons, indifference toward people's needs, a merciless and
blind justice: injustice. *Agape:* a disinterested impulse that leads
us to understand, to empathize, to share, to help, and to heal,
born of faith in the love that God has for us and that we see revealed in our brothers and sisters. That love is still being given
in today's world. As Jerónimo Nadal used to say, it is a flame
that has always been lit, and still is, in the church and in our
least Society, and that we strive to keep alive and quicken. A

flame that is a beacon, a sign of hope, a light for our way, and warmth for our hearts. Love unites, *anomia* divides. Matthew shows these two forces in a permanent state of combat, in an apocalyptic crescendo. *Anomia* is the substantial, historical, and cosmic injustice that undermines the Gospel-inspired basis of human relations. *Agape* is the evangelical message of love and of peace, all that gives meaning to the life that is born of faith, both personal and communitarian or social.

The message of Matthew leaves the door open to hope: "The one who perseveres to the end will be saved" (Matt. 24:13). Persevering despite adverse forces, despite others' incomprehension, despite our own discouragement. In order to overcome, we must persevere in the love of charity that is linked to our faith and calls for the promotion of justice. This charity is the world's only real hope for salvation. To persevere, that is the watchword in Mark's Gospel, too, and in Luke's: "You will be saved if you persevere" (Luke 21:19; see Mark 13:13).

I am firmly convinced that the Society, in virtue of the trinitarian inspiration of its Ignatian charism, rooted and grounded in love, is providentially prepared to enter the struggle and be engaged effectively in curbing the spread of *anomia* and working for the victory of love. The plight of the world, I can confidently assert, so deeply wounds our sensibilities as Jesuits that it sets the inmost fibers of our apostolic zeal a-tingling. Our historical mission is involved in all this, for the purpose of our Society is the defense and propagation of the faith, and we know that faith moves and is moved by charity, and that charity brings about and goes beyond justice. The struggle for faith, the promotion of justice, the commitment to charity, all these are our objective, and in it lies our raison d'être. Our updated renewal consists in letting ourselves be imbued by this idea and in living it with all the intensity of the Ignatian *magis*. In this

way we shall have reached the ultimate source of Ignatius's
trinitarian charism: the divine essence, which is love.

Let me end now greeting you all, as well as every Jesuit who
will read these pages, with that wonderful Pauline formula:
"Peace be to the brethren, and love with faith, from God the
Father and the Lord Jesus Christ. Grace be with all who love
our Lord Jesus Christ with love undying" (Eph. 6:23–24).

— "Rooted and Grounded in Love"
in *SL* 185–88

AN INVOCATION TO THE TRINITY

*Arrupe concludes his important essay "The Trinitarian Inspira-
tion of the Ignatian Charism" with an invocation to the Blessed
Trinity. Like the prayer to Christ Our Model (see p. 108), this
dense prayer draws on numerous passages from Scripture, the
eucharistic liturgy, the Spiritual Exercises, and the life of Ignatius, while interceding on behalf of the Society of Jesus and
the church in the face of numerous contemporary challenges.*

O Most Holy Trinity! Primal mystery, source of everything!
"Who has ever seen him, to give a description? Who can glo-
rify him as he deserves?" (Sir. 43:31) I feel you so sublime, so
far from me, so profound a mystery that I must cry out from
the bottom of my heart, "Holy, holy, holy Lord God of hosts,
heaven and earth are full of your glory. Hosanna in the highest!" The more I feel your inaccessible greatness, the more I feel
my own puniness and nothingness. And yet, plunging deeper
and deeper into the abyss of that nothingness I meet you at the
very depths of my being, loving me, sustaining me so that I will
not lapse back into nothing, working through me, for me, with
me in a mysterious communion of love.

Kneeling before you, I dare to raise my plea, to ask for your wisdom, even though realizing that the summit of a person's knowledge of you means knowing that he or she knows nothing of you. But I also know that the obscurity is suffused with the light of the mystery that eludes me. Give me that "mysterious, hidden wisdom of God, destined since before the ages began to be for our glory" (1 Cor. 2:3).

As a son of Ignatius and called to live his vocation, which you have chosen me for, I ask you for some of that "unusual," "exceptional," "extraordinary" light from the depths of the Trinity, so that I can appreciate the charism of Ignatius, accept it and live it as it should be lived in this historical moment of your Society.

Grant me, Lord, to see everything now with new eyes, to discern and test the spirits that help me read the signs of the times, to relish the things that are yours, and to communicate them to others. Give me the clarity of understanding that you gave Ignatius.

I want you to start treating me, Lord, as a schoolteacher does a child, for I am ready to follow even a little dog (*Autobiography of St. Ignatius*) in order to go the right way.

Let your light be for me like the burning bush for Moses, the light of Damascus for Paul, the Cardoner and La Storta for Ignatius. That is, a call to set out on a road that may be obscure, but that will open up before me, as happened to Ignatius when he was following it.

Grant me that trinitarian light which enabled Ignatius to grasp your mysteries so profoundly that he could write: "There was no more to know in this matter of the Most Holy Trinity." Like him, I want to feel that everything ends in you.

I ask you, also, to teach me the meaning — for me and for the Society — of what you showed Ignatius. Grant that we may learn more and more the treasures of your mystery, which will help us to advance without going astray along the road of the Society, which is our road to you. Convince us that you are the source of our vocation, and that we will achieve far more trying to penetrate your mysteries in contemplation and to live the abundance of divine life than turning to merely human means and activities. We know that our prayer leads us to action and that "no one is helped by you in the Society just for himself" (Nadal).

Like Ignatius, I bend my knees to thank you for this so sublime trinitarian vocation to the Society. Like St. Paul, who also bent his knees before the Father, I beg you to grant to the whole Society that "planted in love and built on love, it will with all the saints have strength to grasp the breadth and the length, the height and the depth" (Eph. 3:18–19), and that, knowing the love of Christ, which is beyond all knowledge, I too may be filled with the utter fullness of you, Most Holy Trinity. Give me your Spirit who "reaches the depths of everything, even the depths of God" (1 Cor. 2:10).

To attain that fullness, I follow the advice of Nadal to put my prayer by preference in "a contemplation of the Trinity, in love and in the union of charity, which includes our neighbors, too, by the ministries of our vocation."

I end with the prayer of Ignatius: "Eternal Father, confirm me; Eternal Son, confirm me; Holy Spirit, confirm me; Holy Trinity, confirm me; my one only God, confirm me."

— "The Trinitarian Inspiration of the
Ignatian Charism" in *SL* 137–39

4

The World

The gospel is a gospel of love. But love demands justice. The gospel is therefore a gospel of justice also. It is the Good News preached to the poor.   —*Pedro Arrupe*

WORLD OF SIN AND GRACE

This section introduces Arrupe's wide-ranging and profound understanding of the faith that does justice. As such it responds to the perennial demands that faith be authentic: What does it mean to be a genuine person of faith and follower of Christ today? What is required of those who would live their faith honestly in this world riven by sin? In the spirit of the "Contemplation on the Incarnation" from the Spiritual Exercises of St. Ignatius, these five selections locate the necessary connection between faith and justice in the deeper relationship between faith and discipleship and, ultimately, in the saving mystery of the cross.

The first selection, **The Social Dimension of Sin,** *introduces an expansive asceticism of the cross in response to social suffering and the social dimension of sin. The second,* **The Eucharist** *and Action for Justice, connects the mysticism of justice to eucharistic spirituality. The Society of Jesus and Racial Discrimination, the third selection, is one part of a letter written by Father Arrupe in 1967 at the height of the civil rights movement to the Jesuits of the United States; it serves not only as a corporate "examination of conscience," but perceptively links the question of racial justice to issues of economic and social justice. The fourth selection examines the Ignatian roots of the Social Commitment of the Society of Jesus. The fifth piece in this section, On the Killing of Five Jesuits, reflects on the real-world cost of the Society's social commitment, the cost of a discipleship that integrates faith and justice.*

The Social Dimension of Sin

There is an aspect of sin, which used to be put less in relief, but whose importance we see today more than ever and whose comprehension can help us to understand better the mystery of the cross, and what is demanded of us today by way of participation in this mystery. In its strictest sense, sin is an act of the personal will, which, called to good by grace, deliberately closes itself to that call under the impulse of selfish attraction. But this human sin, by the inevitable social projection of all that is human, tends to "objectify itself," and in union with the similar sin of others, to establish social structures which perpetuate and protect the selfish attitude of individuals. These structures engender situations difficult for others — in which they can only with difficulty retreat even from the temptation to sin — and they go so far as to make very difficult or even practically impossible the practice of good and the following of the voice of conscience.

Does not that description, unfortunately, fit great aspects or sectors of the social reality of our time? Do not the miseries

of the Third World come from there? The young often feel
it very keenly. That is why they consider hypocritical the di-
atribes against certain individual sins, when these omit these
other greater social sins. They are not right in what they deny,
but right in what they affirm, namely, the existence of that other
greater sin. Every sin ought to be denounced and combated by
those who wish to share in the prophetic vocation of Jesus.
The church and the Society of Jesus ought to be very clear in
the position they take in the face of the grave collective sins
of today.

It is clear, however, that if it is not a question of concrete
personal sin, the remedy is more difficult. Besides, everything is
not resolved by denunciation, unless it is followed with personal
example and with concrete action opposed to sin. "The mystery
of iniquity" is in the world, and it will not leave it tomorrow or
the day after tomorrow. It is necessary to take account of it and
to undertake against it an action that is broad in scope, patient,
and well directed.

Such an action should not neglect any support that the human
sciences and techniques — especially psychology, sociology, economics, and politics — can offer. It is necessary to know how to
cope with the psychological defects of human beings, and remedy them in the measure possible. It is necessary to know how
to convince people that their happiness does not lie in selfishness. It is necessary, however, to know how to reckon with those
cold laws of sociology and economics that emanate from human
selfishness — without remaining prisoner, on the other hand, of
this motif, but trusting that there are in human beings better resources than those we have manifested up to now. It is necessary
to make a prudent effort, combining the techniques of realism
and possibility with the courage essential for renewal. None of
these things can be neglected. But it would be extremely naive

to believe that all that is going to establish order in the world at once, or that it is going to settle it in a definite way.

The way of the cross of Christ continues, then, to open up for us the other way, that of participation in the redemptive suffering. We will all meet it in our life, as Christ met it, however little we may feel ourselves honored to struggle with him against our own selfishness and that of others, and provided that we do not flee like cowards when it knocks at our door. Traditional asceticism has a repertory of concrete forms of mortification, the result of positive research, and has presented them with insistence as exercises of penance and as participation in the cross. We have come to realize today that the important thing is to accept the evil that comes our way and that makes us share, conjointly with our brothers and sisters, in the suffering caused by injustice and selfishness. If we wish to be ready for this participation, we will certainly find it opportune and essential — in addition to the voluntary asceticism which prepares us for it — to accept the suffering that will come to us, with a view to being faithful, as Jesus Christ, to our vocation, and in order to feel our solidarity, with him and as he does, with the suffering endured by humankind.

— "The Jesuit and the Christ of the
Spiritual Exercises" in *OA* 270–72

The Eucharist and Action for Justice

Brothers and Sisters, the world we live in is full of injustice, hatred, and violence. Everywhere we look we are confronted by what the Synod of Bishops described as "a network of domination, oppression, and abuses which stifle freedom and which keep the greater part of humanity from sharing in the building up and enjoyment of a more just and more fraternal world."

Yet we have an answer that gives us hope and joy. It is the Eucharist, the symbol of Christ's love for humanity. The task of the 1975 Eucharistic Congress is to share that love and translate it into effective action. Without some action, will our Eucharistic Congress have any real message for the world? A message, that is, which modern people will listen to and believe in? Without some tangible evidence of our concern for others, what witness can we give? — "The Eucharist and Hunger" in *JF* 179

The Society of Jesus and Racial Discrimination

Race relations and poverty are not necessarily and everywhere two aspects of the same problem. But, as a matter of fact, in the United States the problem of racial discrimination can hardly be considered apart from the problem of poverty. For it is especially among the hundreds of thousands of racially exploited that the poignant description of the poor by my predecessor, Father John Baptist Janssens, in his *Instruction on the Social Apostolate,* October 10, 1949, is distressingly verified. In that Instruction, Father Janssens pleaded with us Jesuits to understand:

> What it means to spend a whole life in humble circumstances, to be a member of the lowest class of humankind, to be ignored and looked down upon by other people; to be unable to appear in public because one does not have decent clothes or the proper social training; to be the means by which others grow rich; to live from day to day on nothing but the most frugal food, and never to be certain about the morrow; to be forced to work either below or above one's strength, amid every danger to health, honor, and purity of soul; to be unemployed for days and months, tormented by idleness and want; to

be unable to bring up one's children in a decent manner, but rather to be forced to expose them to the common dangers of the public streets, to disease and suffering; to mourn many of them who, lacking the tender care which they need, have been snatched off by death in the bloom of their youth; never to enjoy any decent recreation of soul or body; and at the same time to behold about one the very people for whom one works, abounding in riches, enjoying superfluous comforts, devoting themselves to liberal studies and the fine arts, loaded with honors, authority, and praise.

The poor are rightfully demanding fair participation in the benefits of scientific and technological progress. They are seeking earnestly for leaders who will enable them to secure their just share of the earth's bounty — leaders who will deliver them from the misery of perennial poverty and free them to live in the fullness of human dignity. If, in this revolution of rising expectations, they cannot find in the free world the sympathy and the help they need, they may be tempted to turn to other leaders and to other systems inimical to Christian truths and democratic ideals. . . .

It is chastening to recall that, before the Civil War, some American Jesuit houses owned black slaves. It is humbling to remember that until recently, a number of Jesuit institutions did not admit qualified black students, even in areas where civil restrictions against integrated schools did not prevail, and this even in the case of black Catholics. It is embarrassing to note that, up to the present, some of our institutions have effected what seems to be little more than token integration of black students. It is salutary for us to reflect upon these facts.

It is true of course, that in the history of the Society of Jesus in the United States, Jesuits have distinguished themselves in laboring faithfully and effectively with many minority groups. We in the United States have a long and proud record of work with the American Indian, and with the Irish, the Italian, the German, and the Slav immigrants of the nineteenth and early twentieth centuries. At the present time Jesuits are prominently identified with the Puerto Rican apostolate in the New York metropolitan area, and Jesuit activity for the Mexican-Americans in El Paso is worthy of special commendation.

Nevertheless, our record of service to black Americans has fallen far short of what it should have been. Indeed, in recent years there have been great pioneers like Fathers John LaFarge and John Marko, and others who followed them. These American Jesuits, despite misunderstanding and even opposition, sometimes within the Society itself, have accomplished heroic things in their work with black people. But unfortunately our apostolate to black people in the United States has depended chiefly upon the individual initiative and very little upon a corporate effort of the Society. In the era of mass immigration from Europe to the United States, our men gave outstanding service to the exploited poor, to whom they were bound by ethnic and religious ties. But in the intervening decades, as the immigrant groups advanced economically, educationally, politically, and socially, the Society of Jesus tended to become identified more and more with the middle-class, white segment of the population.

It would be a wholesome practice for each of us, individually and as members of Jesuit communities, to examine our consciences and to inquire why so little of our effort in the past has been expended in work for and with black Americans. Permit me to suggest some possible answers: a failure to appreciate fully the practical implications of the Christian concept of the human person; an uncritical acceptance of certain stereotypes and prejudices regarding blacks, acquired in youth and not effectively eradicated by the training in the Society; the insulation of far too many Jesuits from the actual living conditions of the poor, and hence of most black Americans; an unconscious conformity to the discriminatory thought and action patterns of the surrounding white community; an unarticulated fear of the reprisals sometimes visited on those who participate in the active black apostolate; the mistaken notion that, since other priests and religious are serving black people, we may exempt ourselves from the obligation of contributing a major effort to the struggle for interracial justice and charity; a lack of sufficient comprehension that, while the Society of Jesus is committed to the service of all humankind, it is especially committed to the service of Christ's poor. Other considerations will undoubtedly suggest themselves to you from your own study and personal experience.

— "Interracial Apostolate" in *JF* 15–16, 20–21

The Social Commitment of the Society of Jesus

There are two fundamental laws of all spiritual life which St. Ignatius makes his own, putting them at the center of the Spiritual Exercises: the law of charity, of a charity that knows no bounds, and the law of spiritual discernment, a product of prayer and intimacy with God, which helps us to discover where and in what manner, in the concrete circumstances of life, our charity should be manifested: by a love which attests its vigor in making it capable precisely of "discerning."

In general, the foundation of our external activities of charity and justice, which are basic for full human development, is found in an intimate connection, in the theological identification between the vertical dimension and the horizontal dimension of Christian love: this is one and the same charity. It is only through love for God in transcendent Trinity, rendered visible in the person of Christ, that we can explain the perfect love for our fellow human beings that leads us to wish to identify ourselves with them in their sufferings and to wish to come to their rescue.

Christian theology and anthropology, resting in the last analysis on the incarnation, the death, the resurrection, and the eschatological return of Christ, will make us avoid the incomplete horizontalism of a secularized or atheistic philanthropy. They will bring us to the constant reflection necessary to modify the existing social situation when considered unjust. They will make us embody in a horizontal dimension of charity toward the neighbor the vertical relation of our sincere charity toward a personal and transcendent God.

I am not speaking here of charity as distinct from justice but of charity that demands and lays the foundation for justice, which procures justice, and makes it possible by effecting a transformation in the hearts and the mentalities of people — the charity which constitutes the essence of the Gospel message.

In the sphere of the social apostolate we speak, and with reason, of justice, of a just order based on equity. But perhaps there is danger of forgetting that it is in the name of Christian charity and love that we desire this just order, and that we are striving to obtain it.

Discreet charity: this is the watchword for our efforts in this sphere as in all others — but in this sphere especially today. In our day it is impossible to have a genuine charity without feeling a deep preoccupation with the social problems that rend humankind and dehumanize the life of the majority of people. It is impossible to have a genuine charity without hearing the appeal and coming to the rescue. And a discretion which does not discern in the light of the faith the means possible to answer this appeal will no longer avail. Further, it is not only a question of response by individual action, but also and above all by the combined action of the Society.

That is what we mean when we speak of the "social commitment of the Society." In recent ascetical language the word "commitment" has come to signify the same thing as the traditional "devotion" — devotion or gift of self, but emphasizing that we cannot stop at sentiment but we must go on to act. It means that we cannot seek the spiritual solely, but we must embody our commitment in an actual situation — in persons and in real events.

The new conditions of life in the world, characterized today by industrial development, the demographic explosion, and socialization, have made the Christian conscience more sensitive to this appeal to social commitment. The Society of Jesus, thanks to the numerous apostolic enterprises in mission lands, has played the role of pioneer, has had then by anticipation a clear sense of the Christian value of the initiatives of social and human progress. It has then still more reason for feeling concerned today about this appeal.

— "The Social Commitment of the Society of Jesus"
in JF 31–33

On the Killing of Five Jesuits (1976–77)

The recent murder of Father Rutilio Grande, S.J., on March 12, 1977, in the Central American republic of El Salvador seems to me to be a clear sign from the Lord. Father Grande is the fifth victim that God has chosen from our ranks in the past few months. The other victims were Father João Bosco Burnier, S.J., murdered on October 11, 1976, in Brazil, and Fathers Martin Thomas, S.J., Christopher Shepherd-Smith, S.J., and Brother John Conway, S.J., murdered on February 6, 1977, in Rhodesia (Zimbabwe). The Lord speaks to the Society of Jesus through the pouring out of this blood, as through the blood of Abel, as through the blood of Christ on the cross.

Mingled with our deep grief at seeing beloved brothers snatched from our midst is a great happiness, unmistakable proof that through these deaths Jesus Christ has a message for the Society. What is that message? Let us try to fathom it.

Who are the victims that God has chosen? The five were men of average human gifts, leading obscure lives, more or less unrecognized, dwelling in small villages, and totally dedicated to the daily service of the poor and suffering. These were sons of the Society who never took part in broad national controversies and who never made headlines in the news media. Their style of life was simple, austere, evangelical; it was a life that used them up slowly, day-by-day, in the service of "the little ones."

Why did the Lord choose them? I believe it is precisely because of the evangelical life, one that is clearly apostolic and in which the image of a true "companion of Jesus" is never blurred. Their attitudes, their activities, their motives are not colored by ideological or partisan ambiguities. They are men who had learned to put up with misunderstanding and, in a spirit of nonviolence, endeavored to follow the directives of the church and the Society, and above all, to imitate the Good Shepherd. There can be no slightest doubt about the unaffected simplicity of their lives.

They were, therefore, unquestionably following the line of action that the Thirty-second General Congregation marked out for the Society: the service of faith and the promotion of justice. The Lord seems once again to be showing us his preferences and to be pointing out the values and the kind of witness that he holds in great esteem. He has lifted out of obscurity for the whole world to see and crowned with martyrdom these "faithful servants" of his, men who were faithful to him in little and humdrum affairs, men who served him in the hungry, the thirsty, the homeless, men who loved him in the poor by their works and sincerity.

The Lord seems to be showing us, then, what kind of martyr is found in today's world. And the church seems to believe that, too, for in a spontaneous reaction it has not hesitated to label each of their deaths a "martyrdom." Pope Paul VI himself used that word about the victims of Rhodesia; the bishops of Brazil applied it in reference to Father Burnier; and finally, the bishops, the clergy and the people of El Salvador interpreted Father Rutilio Grande's death that way when they thanked God "for having given us the first Salvadoran martyr."

These are Jesuits of the mold that the world and the church need today. Men driven by the love of God to serve their brothers and sisters without distinction of class or race. Men who are able to identify themselves with those who suffer, who live with them, and even give up their own lives on their behalf. Strong men who know how to defend human rights in the Gospel spirit, even to the sacrifice of life itself, it that be necessary (John 15:13).

If we follow Christ, persecution will come, as we have discovered through experience in so many countries when we try to serve faith and promote justice. Not all of us will witness to Christ by shedding our life's blood in sacrifice, but all of us should unreservedly offer him our whole lives. The essential thing, the Jesuit thing, is always to confess him before people. As I said to the General Congregation in December of 1974: "The thing that counts is that we really resolve to follow Christ even without knowing what sacrifice this following of him will certainly demand of us."

To be able to carry out this vocation of ours, the Society today must count on men and on communities imbued with the "mind of Christ," who serve Christ without limit or reservation, who joyfully lead lives of evangelical simplicity and continuing self-sacrifice, thus offering to our contemporaries an ideal for living, and to the generous youth of our day a model and way of life. This is the real secret of success in our mission in the church. This will be the source of new vocations: "the blood of martyrs is the seed of vocations." This is the Jesuit that St. Ignatius, that the pope, and above all that the Eternal King wishes today to find in each one of us.

— "Our Recent Five Third World Martyrs" in *JF* 206–8

THE WORLDWIDE REFUGEE CRISIS

The two selections in this section touch on a concern close to Arrupe's heart: the plight of refugees. **The Society of Jesus and the Refugee Problem** *announces Arrupe's decision as Superior General to establish the Jesuit Refugee Service. The following year, on August 6, 1981, the thirty-sixth anniversary of Hiroshima, Arrupe gave an impromptu address,* **To Jesuits Working with Refugees in Thailand.** *He encourages and exhorts his brother Jesuits to be men of compassion and prayer. This, it turned out, was to be his last public address; upon his return to Rome the next day, he suffered the stroke that left him partially paralyzed and with impaired speech.*

The Society of Jesus and the Refugee Problem

Around Christmas time, last year, struck and shocked by the plight of thousands of boat people and refugees, I felt it my duty to send cable messages to some twenty Major Superiors around the world. Sharing my distress with them, I asked what they in their own countries and the universal society could do to bring at least some relief to such a tragic situation.

Their response was magnificent. Immediate offers of help were made in personnel, know-how, and material; supplies of food and medicine as well as money were sent; direct action was taken through the mass media to influence government and private agencies; services were volunteered in pastoral as well as organizational capacities, and so on....

At the outset, I explained that this situation constitutes a challenge to the Society we cannot ignore if we are to remain faithful to St. Ignatius's criteria for our apostolic work and the recent calls of the Thirty-first and Thirty-second General Congregations. In the *Constitutions* St. Ignatius speaks of the greater universal good, an urgency that is ever growing, the difficulty and complexity of the human problem involved, and lack of other people to attend to the need. With our ideal of availability and universality, the number of institutions under our care, and the active collaboration of many lay people who work with us, we are particularly well-fitted to meet this challenge and provide services that are not being catered for sufficiently by other organizations and groups....Furthermore, the help needed is not only material: in a special way the Society is being called to render a service that is human, pedagogical, and spiritual. It is a difficult and complex challenge; the needs are dramatically urgent. I have no hesitation in repeating what I said at our Consultation: "I consider this as a new modern apostolate for the Society as a whole, of great importance for today and the future, and of much spiritual benefit also to the Society." ...

In the light of our Consultation and after further discussion with my General Counselors, I have decided to set up within the Curia a service to coordinate Jesuit refugee work, which will henceforth be referred to as the *Jesuit Refugee Service* (JRS).... The aims and objectives of JRS are as follows:

1. To set up a network of contacts within the Society so that existing work for refugees can be better planned and coordinated;

2. To collect information that might lead to new opportunities for assistance to refugees;

3. To act as a switchboard between offers of help from Provinces and the needs of international agencies and organizations;

4. To raise the consciousness of the Society about the importance of this apostolate and the different forms it can take both within countries of first asylum and receiving countries;

5. To direct the special attention of the Society toward those groups or areas that receive little publicity or help from elsewhere;

6. To encourage our publications and institutes of learning to undertake research into the root causes of the refugee problem so that preventive action can be taken.

— "The Society of Jesus and the Refugee Problem"
in *EC* 28–29

Address to Jesuits Working with Refugees in Thailand

I am very happy to hear all of the information you have given. It is natural that those working with refugees should have different reactions and points of view. Service to refugees adds a new dimension to your Jesuit work here in Thailand. The international Society can help, but this new development has special implications for you.

First, I want to repeat what Father Bob Rush [the Jesuits' Regional Assistant for East Asia] was saying: I think you should be very happy with your work here. You are doing a wonderful work, though a difficult one. It is an important work. You see little success externally in a country that is mostly Buddhist and where there are so few Catholics. This is the hardest type of missionary apostolate. I think I can speak from experience. In Japan you may find a parish priest baptizing only two people in ten years. Actually, what is in question here is not external success but commitment. We are to work as best we can — as I have been telling members of the Society of Jesus all over the world. The Society has initiative and creativity. But sometimes the way it has used these has meant choosing the easier apostolates. I doubt whether the easy apostolate is the real apostolate!

The apostolate in Thailand is one of the most difficult in the Society because of the cultural conditions, the weather conditions, the political conditions, and all the rest. So you require a great heart to work with enthusiasm in a work whose results you do not see. Those who come after will say: "What a wonderful job we are doing!" But they should not forget the many people who went before preparing the way.

Do not misunderstand me: I can see that you are happy. But I can also see that your work is burdensome. Sometimes when you speak from the heart some feelings come out, not bitter feelings exactly, but ones that result from the burdens of your work — really hard work. And perhaps this is not always recognized by others.

Now it is time to consider the kind of help that the Society can give to the work among refugees. First, this new direction has implications for the Society's work here in Thailand. That is because what I am calling a new dimension will involve collaboration with those Fathers already working in Thailand. As your Father Superior has indicated to me, this will mean an added burden for all. It will mean taking someone away from his present work for what is virtually a full-time new job — while you are so short of people.

I see my commitment, then, as not only to the Thai apostolate as it is now, but also to the new Thai apostolate with the refugees. Because of this new dimension, the Society as a whole should assist the direct work being done by the Jesuits in Thailand.

The other question concerns the new opening possible here. The work for the refugees can, and should, have a great effect on the Society's image in Thailand. And you should benefit greatly from that. But if this is to happen, the decision rests with the Society here in Thailand. We can only start out on this tremendous work step by step, looking ahead and searching out the way. Most probably we shall have to search for it daily.

At present the situation all across the world is changing very greatly. It is difficult, then, to have a fixed plan. A ten-year plan? Oh no, excuse me! If you have a two-year plan that will perhaps be enough, or even a day-to-day plan, because the situation is changing all the time and you are experimenting. And this is where prudence comes in, prudence to take calculated risks. You don't have to be 100 percent certain. In today's world nobody can be 100 percent certain.

For this reason, *a fortiori,* great risks have to be taken in many places. "I made a mistake!" Well, what this means is that we make a communal discernment as a group, and then set a policy. And this policy should be flexible precisely so that we can experiment further. In all of this you have to think and pray as a group if you are to discover a general policy, and principles that everybody will accept. The "elasticity" of this experimentation and risk-taking should be all in one direction — the direction pointed out by the Holy Spirit.

To come to an agreed policy you will have to face tensions, because we have different opinions. Everybody has to express his opinion and his experiences clearly. And at the end there has to be a conclusion of some kind. Perhaps someone will have to change his opinion, or at least act according to the opinion of someone else. That is the price we have to pay.

I have learned many things today. For example, we talked about the local church. But we have to *be* the local church! (Excuse me for telling you that.) When the Society comes to work in a new area, the first reaction of others is to be wary. The Society is feared everywhere: "These Jesuits are very shrewd. They are powerful." As I was saying the other day at the Ateneo de Manila: we are not as bad as people say we are, nor are we as good as people think we are. We are normal in that we are not geniuses. Perhaps we have a few geniuses in the Society, but very few. Years ago it was said that the great power the Society possesses is its well-trained mediocrity!

And unity? Yes, that is important. We share the same spirituality and the same commitment to Christ. "Excellence," as St. Ignatius thinks of it, is not scholarly excellence, though it may include that. Real excellence lies in commitment to Christ. We have to be excellent in our commitment.

Perhaps what Father Ando Isamu was saying is utopian, but how terrific it would be for the Society to have non-Christians coming to work for the poor in the villages — coming motivated by philanthropy. If we could create a situation of that kind, we would have enormous possibilities for our work in Thailand. Then we would be collaborating with people to much greater effect than we can through those few Catholics that we are in the Orient. And through the mass media we can present matters in a human way, and so multiply the work and its effects. In that way we can build up the country indirectly.

This would amount to preevangelization done by non-Christians! Yet in fact, by definition, we do not speak about Christ during preevangelization. We cannot speak about Christ, but we have non-Christians doing something out of good will that we could do. I see an opening within refugee work for such an apostolate. I think this will be good to think about.

Now to the question of a coordinator for the apostolate among the refugees: I think this matter has to be decided here in Thailand. It is necessary to have somebody full-time to consider all the things we have discussed. He has to be a man who can hear opinions. He cannot give first place to his own personal opinion as an individual. The situation will be very complex in the beginning. The coordinator has to have an ear for every one of you and for those who come from regions outside Thailand, for the bishops here and for everything that is going on. After that he will consult with the superior of the place and settle the policy to be followed. He has to be a very good man, open and prudent, and with courage. This is because, although he is dependent on the local superior for final decisions, he will be the one who executes the policy.

I am very happy. I see a tremendous opening for the Society, and not only as regards work among refugees. This work will be a school in which we learn many things.

I will tell you something I ask myself very often: Should we give spiritual help to the guerrillas in Latin America? No, you say? Well, I cannot say no. Perhaps in the past I have. But they are human beings, souls who are suffering. If you have a wounded person, even if he is a guerrilla you have to help him. That is the meaning of being a Good Samaritan. Is this political? People say so. But no, I am being a priest now. I am helping this poor person. I don't care if he is a guerrilla, a religious, or a non-Catholic. He is a poor person. He is the poor person who is suffering.

We cannot be naive and allow ourselves to be used politically by other people. But on the other hand we need a real Christian commitment. So many in Latin America are helping other people — perhaps guerrillas among them — taking them into their homes in order to save them from being killed. Charity is one thing, principle another, and casuistry is a third. Actual cases can be very difficult to resolve.

Still, we have to be open to many things. We are close to limits here — not only to the limits of Cambodia and Thailand. We are close to the limits of morality and of our own positions. We have to be careful.

For me it was a very consoling experience to write the letter about Communism and Social Analysis. In that letter, I said that sometimes we have to collaborate with Communists. I cited *Populorum progressio,* paragraph 23, as a reference. Why? Because I think what it says is true. But people will be scandalized! True, but that is what the Holy Father is telling us, so I am safe.

Take the case of Ethiopia. There we have a university, once Catholic, which was taken over by a Communist government. The Holy Father has told me to send Jesuits to the University of Asmara, a Communist university. So we are collaborating with the Communists by order of the Holy Father. Wonderful! We are not going there because we think we can influence many people in Ethiopia. We are going without supporting any Communist ideology.

Situations such as these are very difficult and complicated. Everything must be done with great discernment. It is not enough to have a great idea one day and go straight ahead and act on it. No, that could be very bad — unless the person in question is a prophetic servant inspired with a wonderful idea. The mixture of prophecy and prudence, security and risk, makes for complex situations. In Thailand you are in one of the hottest spots in this regard. Courage, please!

I will say one more thing, and please don't forget it. Pray. Pray much. Problems such as these are not solved by human efforts. I am telling you things that I want to emphasize, a message — perhaps my "swan song" — for the Society. We pray at the beginning and at the end — we are good Christians! But in our three-day meetings, if we spend half a day in prayer about the conclusions we expect to come to, or about our points of view, we will have very different "lights." And we will come to quite different syntheses — in spite of different points of view — ones we could never find in books nor arrive at through discussion.

Right here we have a classic case: If we are indeed in the front line of a new apostolate in the Society, we have to be enlightened by the Holy Spirit. These are not the pious words of a novice master. What I am saying is 100 percent from St. Ignatius. When I decided to come to Thailand, they said I could visit refugee camps. I have been in camps before. What we have done here is much more important. I am so happy, and I think it is providential that I came here.

There has to be a basic unity of minds for this new type of apostolate just about to be born. What we are going through here is the birth pangs before this new apostolate can be born. With this medical observation I conclude my talk!

— "Final Address to Jesuits Working with Refugees
in Thailand" in *EC 6*

MEN AND WOMEN FOR OTHERS

On the Feast of St. Ignatius, July 31, 1973, while in Valencia, Spain, Arrupe gave one of his most famous speeches. His audience was comprised of the alumni of Jesuit schools from various

parts of Europe, many of whom came from wealthy and pres-
tigious families. His horizon included the landmark document
of the 1971 Synod of Bishops, "Justice in the World." Early in
his talk, Arrupe asked his audience whether their Jesuit teach-
ers had adequately educated them for justice. He then observed,
"You and I know what many of your Jesuit teachers will answer
to that question. They will answer, in all sincerity and humility:
'No, we have not.'"

A generation later, one cannot help but notice that a pal-
pable shift in Jesuit life and ministry has taken place. The
task of "educating men and women for others" has become
almost a byword in the various circles of Jesuit education.
Many Jesuit schools now promote some version of this saying
as an official or unofficial motto, and changes in the cur-
ricula and campus ministries of the schools reflect the shift
to justice-centered evangelization. The Thirty-second General
Congregation of the Society of Jesus, which Arrupe called and
over which he presided in 1974–75, declared: "The mission of
the Society of Jesus today is the service of faith, of which the
promotion of justice is an absolute requirement." This, perhaps
more than anything else, represents the defining achievement
of his term as Superior General of the Society of Jesus. His
address, "Men and Women for Others," remains a striking re-
minder and symbol of that achievement. Originally titled "Men
for Others" but later emended by Arrupe himself, his remarks
are reproduced here in their entirety.

Education for justice has become in recent years one of the chief
concerns of the church. Why? Because there is a new awareness in the church that participation in the promotion of justice
and the liberation of the oppressed is a constitutive element
of the mission which Our Lord has entrusted to her. Impelled

by this awareness, the church is now engaged in a massive effort to educate — or rather to reeducate — herself, her children, and all men and women so that we may all "lead our life in its entirety...in accord with the evangelical principles of personal and social morality to be expressed in a living Christian witness."

Today our prime educational objective must be to form men-and-women-for-others; men and women who will live not for themselves but for God and his Christ — for the God-human who lived and died for all the world; men and women who cannot even conceive of love of God which does not include love for the least of their neighbors; men and women completely convinced that love of God which does not issue in justice for others is a farce.

This kind of education goes directly counter to the prevailing educational trend practically everywhere in the world. We Jesuits have always been heavily committed to the educational apostolate. We still are. What, then, shall we do? Go with the current or against it? I can think of no subject more appropriate than this for the General of the Jesuits to take up with the former students of Jesuit schools.

First, let me ask this question: Have we Jesuits educated you for justice? You and I know what many of your Jesuit teachers will answer to that question. They will answer, in all sincerity and humility: No, we have not. If the terms "justice" and "education for justice" carry all the depth of meaning which the church gives them today, we have not educated you for justice.

What is more, I think you will agree with this self-evaluation, and with the same sincerity and humility acknowledge that you have not been trained for the kind of action for justice and witness to justice which the church now demands of us. What does this mean? It means that we have work ahead of us. We must help each other to repair this lack in us, and above all make sure that in future the education imparted in Jesuit schools will be equal to the demands of justice in the world.

It will be difficult, but we can do it. We can do it because, despite our historical limitations and failures, there is something which lies at the very center of the Ignatian spirit, and which enables us to renew ourselves ceaselessly and thus to adapt ourselves to new situations as they arise.

What is this something? It is the spirit of constantly seeking the will of God. It is that sensitiveness to the Spirit which enables us to recognize where, in what direction, Christ is calling us at different periods of history, and to respond to that call.

This is not to lay any prideful claim to superior insight or intelligence. It is simply our heritage from the Spiritual Exercises of St. Ignatius. For these Exercises are essentially a method enabling us to make very concrete decisions in accordance with God's will. It is a method that does not limit us to any particular option, but spreads out before us the whole range of practicable options in any given situation. It opens up for us a sweeping vision embracing many possibilities, to the end that God himself, in all his tremendous originality, may trace out our path for us.

It is this "indifference," in the sense of lack of differentiation, this not being tied down to anything except God's will, that gives to the Society and to the men and women it has been privileged to educate what we may call their multifaceted potential, their readiness for anything, any service that may be demanded of them by the signs of the times.

Jesuit education in the past had its limitations. It was conditioned by time and place. As a human enterprise it will always be. But it could not have been a complete failure if we were able to pass on to you this spirit of openness to new challenges, this readiness for change, this willingness — putting it in Scriptural terms — to undergo conversion. This is our hope: that we have educated you to listen to the living God, to read the Gospel so as always to find new light in it, to think with the church, within which the Word of God always ancient, ever new, resounds with that precise note and timbre needed by each historical epoch. For this is what counts. On this is founded our confidence for the future.

It is not as a father speaking to children that I speak to you today. It is as a companion, a fellow alumnus, speaking to his classmates. Sitting together on the same school bench, let us together listen to the Lord, the Teacher of all humankind.

What Kind of Justice? What Kind of Person? There are two lines of reflection before us. One is to deepen our understanding of the idea of justice as it becomes more and more clear in the light of the Gospel and the signs of the times. The other is to determine the character and quality of the type of people we want to form, the type of man or woman into which we must be changed, and toward which the generations succeeding us must be encouraged to develop, if we and they are to serve this evangelical ideal of justice.

The first line of reflection begins with the Synod of Bishops of 1971 and its opening statement on "Justice in the World":

Gathered from the whole world, in communion with all who believe in Christ and with the entire human family, and opening our hearts to the Spirit who is making the whole of creation new, we have questioned ourselves about the mission of the People of God to further justice in the world.

Scrutinizing the "signs of the times" and seeking to detect the meaning of emerging history...we have listened to the Word of God that we might be converted to the fulfilling of the divine plan for the salvation of the world....

We have...been able to perceive the serious injustices
which are building around the world of men and women
a network of domination, oppression, and abuses which
stifle freedom and which keep the greater part of humanity
from sharing in the building up and enjoyment of a more
just and more fraternal world.

At the same time we have noted the inmost stirring
moving the world in its depths. There are facts con-
stituting a contribution to the furthering of justice. In
associations of men and women and among peoples there
is arising a new awareness which spurs them on to liberate
themselves and to be responsible for their own destiny.

Please note that these words are not a mere repetition of
what the church has traditionally taught. They are not a re-
finement of doctrine at the level of abstract theory. They are
the resonance of an imperious call of the living God asking
his church and all persons of good will to adopt certain attitudes and undertake certain types of action which will enable
them effectively to come to the aid of humankind oppressed
and in agony.

This interpretation of the signs of the times did not origi-
nate with the Synod. It began with the Second Vatican Council.
Its application to the problem of justice was made with considerable vigor in *Populorum progressio*. And spreading outward
from this center to the ends of the earth, it was taken up in
1968 by the Latin American bishops at Medellín, in 1969 by
the African bishops at Kampala, in 1970 by the Asian bishops in Manila. In 1971, Pope Paul VI gathered all these voices
together in the great call to action of *Octogesima adveniens*.

The bishops of the Synod took it one step further, and in
words of the utmost clarity said: "Action on behalf of justice and participation in the transformation of the world fully

appear to us as a constitutive dimension of the preaching of the Gospel, or, in other words, of the church's mission for the redemption of the human race and its liberation from every oppressive situation." We cannot, then, separate action for justice and liberation from oppression from the proclamation of the Word of God.

This is plain speech indeed. However, it did not prevent doubts, questionings, even tensions from arising within the church itself. It would be naïve not to recognize this fact. Contradictions, or at least dichotomies, have emerged regarding the actual implementation of this call to action, and our task now is to try to harmonize these dichotomies if we can. This would be in the spirit of the Holy Year that is coming, which is the spirit of reconciliation.

To begin with, let us note that these dichotomies are differences of stress rather than contradictions of ideas. In view of the present call to justice and liberation, where should we put our stress — in our attitudes, our activities, our lifestyle — on justice among persons, or justice before God? on love of God, or love of the neighbor? on Christian charity or human justice? on personal conversion or social reform? on liberation in this life or salvation in the life to come? on development through the inculcation of Christian values, or development through the application of scientific technologies and social ideologies?

1. Quite clearly, the mission of the church is not coextensive with the furthering of justice on this planet. Still, the furthering of justice is a constitutive element of that mission, as the Synod teaches. Recall the Old Testament: that first covenant, the pact of God with his chosen people, was basically concerned with the carrying out of justice, to such a degree that the violation of justice as it concerns people implies a rupture of the covenant with God. Turn, now, to the New Testament, and see how Jesus has received from his Father the mission to bring

the Good News to the poor, liberation to the oppressed, and to make justice triumph. "Blessed are the poor" — why? Because the Kingdom has already come; the Liberator is at hand.

2. We are commanded to love God and to love our neighbor. But note what Jesus says: the second commandment is like unto the first; they fuse together into one compendium of the Law. And in his vision of the Last Judgment, what does the Judge say? "As long as you did this for one of the least of my brothers or sisters, you did it for me" (Matt. 25:40). As Father Alfaro says:

> Inclusion in or expulsion from the Kingdom proclaimed by Jesus depends on our attitude toward the poor and oppressed; toward those who are identified in Isaiah 58:1–2 as the victims of human injustice and in whose regard God wills to realize his justice. What is strikingly new here is that Jesus makes these despised and marginalized folk his brothers. He identifies himself with the poor and the powerless, with all who are hungry and miserable. Every person in this condition is Christ's brother or sister; that is why what is done for them is done for Christ himself. Whoever comes effectively to the aid of these brothers and sisters of Jesus belongs to his Kingdom; whoever abandons them to their misery excludes himself or herself from that Kingdom.[1]

3. Just as love of God, in the Christian view, fuses with love of neighbor, to the point that they cannot possibly be separated, so, too, charity and justice meet together and in practice are identical. How can you love someone and treat that person unjustly? Take justice away from love and you destroy love. You do not have love if the beloved is not seen as a person whose

---

1. Juan B. Alfaro, S.J., *Christianisme et Justice* (Vatican City: Pontifical Commission for Justice and Peace, 1973), 28.

dignity must be respected, with all that that implies. And even if you take the Roman notion of justice as giving to each his due, what is owing to him, Christians must say that we owe love to all people, enemies not excepted.

Just as we are never sure that we love God unless we love others, so we are never sure that we have love at all unless our love issues in works of justice. And I do not mean works of justice in a merely individualistic sense. I mean three things: first, a basic attitude of respect for all people which forbids us ever to use them as instruments for our own profit; second, a firm resolve never to profit from, or allow ourselves to be suborned by, positions of power deriving from privilege, for to do so, even passively, is equivalent to active oppression. To be drugged by the comforts of privilege is to become contributors to injustice as silent beneficiaries of the fruits of injustice; third, an attitude not simply of refusal but of counterattack against injustice; a decision to work with others toward the dismantling of unjust social structures so that the weak, the oppressed, the marginalized of this world may be set free.

4. Sin is not only an act, a personal act, which makes us personally guilty. Over and above this, sin reaches out to what we may call the periphery of ourselves, vitiating our habits, customs, spontaneous reactions, criteria and patterns of thought, imagination, will. And it is not only ourselves who influence our "periphery." It is shaped by all who have helped to form us, by all who form part of our world.

We thus have a congenital inclination toward evil. In theological language this is called "concupiscence," which is, concretely, a combination in us of the sin of Adam and all the sins in history — including our own. When we are converted, when God effects in us the marvel of justification, we turn to God and our brothers and sisters in our innermost selves, and as a consequence sin in the strict sense is washed away from us. However, the effects of sin continue their powerful domination over our "periphery," and this, quite often, in a way that we are not even aware of.

Now, Christ did not come merely to free us from sin and flood the center of our person with his grace. He came to win our entire self for God — including what I have called our "periphery." Christ came to do away not only with sin, but with its effects, even in this life; not only to give us his grace, but to show forth the power of his grace.

Let us see the meaning of this as it pertains to the relationship between personal conversion and structural reform. If "personal conversion" is understood in the narrow sense of justification operative only at the very core of our person, it does not adequately represent the truth of the matter, for such justification is only the root, the beginning of a renewal, a reform of the structures at the "periphery" of our being, not only personal but social.

If we agree on this, conclusions fairly tumble forth. For the structures of this world — our customs; our social, economic, and political systems; our commercial relations; in general, the institutions we have created for ourselves — insofar as they have injustice built into them, are the concrete forms in which sin is objectified. They are the consequences of our sins throughout history, as well as the continuing stimulus and spur for further sin.

There is a biblical concept for this reality. It is what St. John calls, in a negative sense, the "world." The "world" is in the social realm what "concupiscence" is in the personal, for, to use the classical definition of concupiscence, it "comes from sin and inclines us to it."

Hence, like concupiscence, the "world" as understood in this sense must also be the object of our efforts at purification. Our new vision of justice must give rise to a new kind of spirituality, of asceticism; or rather, an expansion of traditional spirituality and asceticism to include not only the personal but the social. In short, interior conversion is not enough. God's grace calls us not only to win back our whole selves for God, but to win back our whole world for God. We cannot separate personal conversion from structural social reform.

5. It follows that this purification, this social asceticism, this earthly liberation is so central in our Christian attitude toward life that whoever hold themselves aloof from the battle for justice implicitly refuse love for their fellows and consequently for God. The struggle for justice will never end. Our efforts will never be fully successful in this life. This does not mean that such efforts are worthless.

God wants such partial successes. They are the first-fruits of the salvation wrought by Jesus. They are the signs of the coming of his Kingdom, the visible indications of its mysterious spreading among us. Of course, partial successes imply partial failures; painful failures; the defeat of many people, many of us, who will be overcome and destroyed in the fight against this "world." For this "world" will not take it lying down, as the vivid American expression has it. It will persecute, it will try to exterminate those who do not belong to it and stand in opposition to it.

But this defeat is only apparent. It is precisely those who suffer persecution for the sake of justice who are blessed. It is precisely the crucified who pass through the world "doing good and healing all" (Acts 10:38).

6. To point out in very general fashion that there are injustices in the world — something which everybody knows without being told — that is not enough: agreed. Having stated principles, we must go to a map of the world and point out the critical points — geographical, sociological, cultural — where sin and injustice find their lodgment: also agreed. To do this,

technologies are needed as instruments of analysis and action, and ideologies are needed to program analysis and action so that they will actually dislodge and dismantle injustice: by all means agreed.

What role is left, then, for the inculcation of Christian values, for the Christian ethos? This: we cannot forget that technologies and ideologies, necessary though they are, derive their origin, historically, from a mixture of good and evil. Injustice of one kind or another finds in them too a local habitation and a name.

Put it this way: they are tools, imperfect tools. And it is the Christian ethos, the Christian vision of values, that must use these tools while submitting them to judgment and relativizing their tendency to make absolutes of themselves. Relativizing them, putting them in their place, as it were, with full realization that the Christian ethos cannot possibly construct a new world without their assistance.

With this background, let us now enter upon our second line of reflection, which bears on the formation of men and women who will reconcile these antitheses and thus advance the cause of justice in the modern world; their continuing formation, in the case of us "old timers," their basic formation, in the case of the youth who will hopefully take up the struggle when we can do no more.

With regard to continuing education, let me say this: our alumni associations are called upon, in my opinion, to be a channel par excellence for its realization. Look upon it as your job, and, with the assistance of our Jesuits in the educational apostolate, work out concrete plans and programs for it.

And let us not have too limited an understanding of what continuing education is. It should not be simply the updating of technical or professional knowledge, or even the reeducation necessary to meet the challenges of a rapidly changing world. It should rather be what is most specific in Christian education:

a call to conversion. And that means, today, a conversion that will prepare us for witnessing to justice as God gives us to see it from the signs of our times.

The Men and Women the Church Needs Today. What kind of man or woman is needed today by the church, by the world? One who is a "man-for-others," a "woman-for-others." That is my shorthand description. A man-or-woman-for-others. But does this not contradict the very nature of the human person? Are we not each a "being-for-ourselves"? Gifted with intelligence that endows us with power, do we not tend to control the world, making ourselves its center? Is this not our vocation, our history?

Yes. Gifted with conscience, intelligence, and power each of us is indeed a center. But a center called to go out of ourselves, to give ourselves to others in love — love, which is our definitive and all-embracing dimension, that which gives meaning to all our other dimensions. Only those who love fully realize themselves as persons. To the extent that any of us shut ourselves off from others we do not become more a person; we become less.

Those who live only for their own interests not only provide nothing for others. They do worse. They tend to accumulate in exclusive fashion more and more knowledge, more and more power, more and more wealth; thus denying, inevitably to those weaker than themselves their proper share of the God-given means for human development.

What is it to humanize the world if not to put it at the service of humankind? But egoists not only do not humanize the material creation; they dehumanize others. They change others into things by dominating them, exploiting them, and taking to themselves the fruit of their labor.

The tragedy of it all is that by doing this, egoists dehumanize themselves. They surrender themselves to the possessions they covet. They become their slave — no longer persons who are self-possessed but un-persons, things driven by their blind desires and their objects.

But when we dehumanize, depersonalize ourselves in this way, something stirs within us. We feel frustrated. In our heart of hearts we know that what we have is nothing compared with what we are, what we can be, what we would like to be. We would like to be ourselves. But we dare not break the vicious circle. We think we can overcome our frustrations by striving to have more, to have more than others, to have ever more and more. We thus turn our lives into a competitive rat-race without meaning.

The downward spiral of ambition, competition, and self-destruction twists and expands unceasingly, with the result that we are chained ever more securely to a progressive, and progressively frustrating, dehumanization.

Dehumanization of ourselves and dehumanization of others. For by thus making egoism a way of life, we translate it, we objectify it, in social structures. Starting from our individual sins of egoism, we become exploiters of others, dehumanizing them and ourselves in the process, and hardening the process into a structure of society which may rightfully be called sin objectified. For it becomes hardened in ideas, institutions, impersonal and depersonalized organisms which now escape our direct control, a tyrannical power of destruction and self-destruction.

How escape from this vicious circle? Clearly, the whole process has its root in egoism — in the denial of love. But to try to live in love and justice in a world whose prevailing climate is egoism and injustice, where egoism and injustice are built into the very structures of society — is this not a suicidal, or at least a fruitless undertaking?

And yet, it lies at the very core of the Christian message. It is the sum and substance of the call of Christ. St. Paul put it in a single sentence: "Do not allow yourself to be overcome by evil, but rather, overcome evil with good" (Rom. 12:21). This teach-ing, which is identical with the teaching of Christ about love for the enemy, is the touchstone of Christianity. All of us would like to be good to others, and most of us would be relatively good in a good world. What is difficult is to be good in an evil world, where the egoism of others and the egoism built into the institutions of society attack us and threaten to annihilate us.

Under such conditions, the only possible reaction would seem to be to oppose evil with evil, egoism with egoism, hate with hate; in short, to annihilate the aggressor with his own weapons. But is it not precisely thus that evil conquers us most thoroughly? For then, not only does it damage us exteriorly, it perverts our very heart. We allow ourselves, in the words of St. Paul, to be overcome by evil.

No. Evil is overcome only by good, hate by love, egoism by generosity. It is thus that we must sow justice in our world. To be just, it is not enough to refrain from injustice. One must go further and refuse to play its game, substituting love for self-interest as the driving force of society.

All this sounds very nice, you will say, but isn't it just a little bit up in the air? Very well, let us get down to cases. How do we get this principle of justice through love down to the level of reality, the reality of our daily lives? By cultivating in ourselves three attitudes:

First, a firm determination to live much more simply — as individuals, as families, as social groups — and in this way to stop short, or at least to slow down, the expanding spiral of luxurious living and social competition. Let us have men and women who will resolutely set themselves against the tide of our consumer society. Men and women who, instead of feeling compelled to acquire everything that their friends have will do away with many of the luxuries which in their social set have become necessities, but which the majority of humankind must do without. And if this produces surplus income, well and good; let it be given to those for whom the necessities of life are still luxuries beyond their reach.

Second, a firm determination to draw no profit whatever from clearly unjust sources. Not only that, but going further, to diminish progressively our share in the benefits of an economic and social system in which the rewards of production accrue to those already rich, while the cost of production lies heavily on the poor. Let there be men and women who will bend their energies not to strengthen positions of privilege, but to the extent possible reduce privilege in favor of the underprivileged. Please do not conclude too hastily that this does not pertain to you, that you do not belong to the privileged few in your society. It touches everyone of a certain social position, even though only in certain respects, and even if we ourselves may be the victims of unjust discrimination by those who are even better off than ourselves. In this matter, our basic point of reference must be the truly poor, the truly marginalized, in our own countries and in the Third World.

Third, and most difficult: a firm resolve to be agents of change in society, not merely resisting unjust structures and arrangements, but actively undertaking to reform them. For, if we set out to reduce income insofar as it is derived from participation in unjust structures, we will find out soon enough that we are faced with an impossible task unless those very structures are changed.

Thus, stepping down from our own posts of power would be too simple a course of action. In certain circumstances it may be the proper thing to do; but ordinarily it merely serves to hand over the entire social structure to the exploitation of the egotistical. Here precisely is where we begin to feel how difficult is the struggle for justice; how necessary it is to have recourse to technical ideological tools. Here is where cooperation among alumni and alumni associations becomes not only useful but necessary.

Let us not forget, especially, to bring into our counsels our alumni who belong to the working class. For in the last analysis, it is the oppressed who must be the principal agents of change. The role of the privileged is to assist them, to reinforce with pressure from above the pressure exerted from below on the structures that need to be changed.

Men-and-women-for-others: the paramount objective of Jesuit education — basic, advanced, and continuing — must now be to form such men and women. For if there is any substance in our reflections, then this is the prolongation into the modern world of our humanist tradition as derived from the Spiritual Exercises of St. Ignatius. Only by being a man-or-woman-for-others does one become fully human, not only in the merely natural sense, but in the sense of being the "spiritual" person of St. Paul. The person filled with the Spirit; and we know whose Spirit that is: the Spirit of Christ, who gave his life for the salvation of the world; the God who, by becoming a human person, became, beyond all others, a Man-for-others, a Woman-for-others.　　— "Men and Women for Others" in *JF* 123–38

FACING THE WORLD TWENTY-FIVE YEARS AFTER HIROSHIMA

In 1950, five years after an atomic bomb destroyed the Japanese city of Hiroshima, Pedro Arrupe detailed the massive destruction of that event from the unique perspective of an eyewitness (see p. 39). In 1970, as General of the Society of Jesus, he revisited this awesome event, using it to set the scene for a collective examination of conscience in the face of our troubled world. In this extraordinary reflection, he moves beyond the role of "survivor of Hiroshima" in order to apprehend the enduring apocalyptic dimension of the postwar world. Now, more than half a century removed from the bombing of Hiroshima, this reflection continues to evoke the sense of spiritual crisis latent in the signs of the times today.

The roof tiles, bits of glass, and beams had scarcely ceased falling, and the deafening roar died away, when I rose from the ground and saw before me the wall clock still hanging in its place but motionless. Its pendulum seemed nailed down. It was ten minutes past eight.

For me that silent and motionless clock has been a symbol. The explosion of the first atomic bomb has become a para-historical phenomenon. It is not a memory, it is a perpetual experience, outside history, which does not pass with the ticking of the clock. The pendulum stopped and Hiroshima has remained engraved on my mind. It has no relation with time. It belongs to motionless eternity.

Sad eternity. A constant presence of that human tragedy. Human? No, inhuman, not merely because it spelled indiscriminate destruction of tens of thousands of lives, but also because it continues to torment humanity as an omen of the possible self-destruction of humanity, a humanity that glories in itself. It seemed that this was the surpassing scientific conquest: possession of that great annihilating power so to be feared that nobody would dare to disturb the peace. All the same, a political policy or an ideology may at bottom be even more tragic and annihilating, since its effects, though slower, are more profoundly destructive. Atomic energy is not the most terrible of energies: there are others more terrible still. Atomic disintegration would not have to be feared if it were not at the service of a humanity disintegrated by hate.

1945: twenty-five years ago: the year of the happening. Sometime later I circled the globe for eighteen months, relating what I had seen and lived through. There was no need for me to use rhetorical flourishes to move the thousands and thousands who crowded to hear the "survivor of Hiroshima." Five years later I again went round the western world repeating the same message, and I was heard with the same interest. In 1955 I once more returned to the West and was still heard with the same emotion. And yet again, in 1962, seventeen years after the tragedy, people continued to listen to me and were greatly moved by what they heard.

Times beyond number, so frequently as to be almost nauseating, came the question: "What did you feel at that moment? It must have been terrible." "Terrible? Yes and no." A shock in time of war, a terrible explosion of extraordinary power, these always leave an impression. For me, at that first moment, it was just one more explosion. What did we know of the atomic bomb? We were ignorant of what that solitary B-29 had carefully laid, at a height of 1700 feet, in the semi-transparent atmosphere, on that cloudy August morning. It is unbelievable but true that my feelings were much deeper five years later in Bogotá, when I saw the film *Hiroshima Mon Amour,* a faithful reproduction of that fateful August morning. In one and a half hours there was placed before me on the screen all that was horrifying and tragic in my own experience which had extended over many months. Tears clouded my eyes. I could take no more. I rose from my chair. It was too much for me. All that I had lived in small daily doses of reality, minute by minute, during six months in Hiroshima, was too concentrated on the screen to be relived in an hour. What a humiliating paradox! What I had borne in living reality overpowered me when I saw it on the screen. My nerves, which I was beginning to think were made of iron, melted before that emotional charge.

How much time teaches us. History is the teacher of life, but only on condition that we know how to read her lessons. The oven of Hiroshima has become a fixed satellite in the stratosphere, accompanying the earth in its course round the sun. It is like a latter-day Sword of Damocles hanging over humankind. Its sinister light, capable of destroying the retina of anyone staring it in the face, is an illuminating and discriminating power greater than that of the X-ray. In the midst of so much destruction, confusion, and corruption, the dark mystery of atomic radiation renders the screen of humanity clarescent, revealing both the fleshly futility of that which disappears like a shadow, and the solidity, firmer than bone, of spiritual values. A frontier situation that transposes values. Atomic energy in destroying matter discloses its instability, while making the spirit stand out with its features more strongly pronounced.

Now yet another explosion is breeding in the womb of time, as millions die from hunger and subhuman existence. More than half the human family is undernourished. Day by day the condition of the marginal sections of the peoples of the underdeveloped nations grows more unbearable. And who is responsible for this state of affairs? I do not think that a "sin" of this kind can be attributed to a few persons only. Rather a sizeable part of the human family is at fault.

Clearly the present world order is based neither on justice nor love, but almost always on personal and national interest. The balance of power is a balance of terror. The problem is so complicated that it cannot be solved by individual effort alone. People of good will see that they are bound hand and foot by collectivity. How often have I talked with people who have the very best intentions regarding the economic and social problems of humanity and have heard expressions like the following: "Yes, surely Father, you're right. I would like to do something myself, but I'm responsible to thousands of shareholders who

want ample dividends"; or "I'm in complete agreement with
you, Father, but if we conduct our business in a completely just
way, we won't be able to compete with others who exploit their
work force." Humanity is trapped in a net of steel out of which
it is difficult to break. One hears the candid statement that
only two possibilities exist: either a striking personal conversion
of those who have most influence to bring about the needed
changes, or the violent tearing down of unjust structures.

My own conviction is that violence is not the right way to
get positive results. If that is true, the only thinkable alternative
is the other: namely, the personal conversion of those who have
power and influence. Even so we cannot overlook the fact that
the explosive energy which has been building up in the hearts of
the dispossessed, and been fed by transistor radio and television
news, is an undeniable reality. The transistor radio can serve
in today's world as a means of instruction, but it can also be
a source of explosive power, more powerful indeed than atomic
energy itself; for the latter is blind and subject to human control
while the former is human and therefore gifted with intelligence
and freedom. Once let loose it is practically uncontrollable.

I do not wish to overlook one point which the West seems to
underrate or tries to ignore. It is that the West, with its superiority complex, gives the impression of despising the two-thirds
of the human family who live in the East. These are intelligent
people, moderate in their habits, hardworking, with ancient and
lofty cultural gifts, a profound philosophy of life, and an almost
unlimited capacity for sacrifice and suffering. Their human energies are colossal. The East is keenly sensitive to this Western
attitude, and, in turn, in the depths of its soul, it despises much
of the West. What attempts does the West make to come closer
to the East in a human and constructive way? Perhaps it regards
Asia in the same way as Africa. Not infrequently, developing

countries are convinced that the aid they receive from the industrialized nations is directed first and foremost to the profit of the "donor." The expropriation of foreign assets and the limitations placed on foreign capital are surely a reaction to this. The relationships existing between many countries certainly do not lead to mutual comprehension and the kind of cooperation which might give birth to joint efforts of immense fruitfulness. Rather they increase the tensions between peoples. Could it not be that this will lead some day to an explosion of indignation on the part of two-thirds of humankind?

Another scar of our times is racial discrimination. That the value of a person or a people should be judged by the color of their skin and that, two-thirds of the way into the twentieth century, human rights should be linked to the epidermis is really inconceivable. But it is a reality, and one with incalculable power to destroy. Established great powers and tomorrow's nations are today submitted to a fratricidal struggle in which a brother or sister of color is looked upon as an outsider. His or her views are thought of as those of a guerrilla, and though each individual outburst of protest does not in itself lead to great destruction, it does reveal the strong pressures which this kind of injustice is building up and hints at the unforeseen consequences that perhaps lie ahead.

The "explosive" attitude of young people is another element which cannot be overlooked or neglected. They are often extraordinarily alive to and aware of the situation in today's world. In their sincerity and through their lack of experience they may oversimplify the problems, but their intuition goes to the heart of these matters. They feel almost by instinct a sense of solidarity with those who are oppressed or suffering. They feel that they themselves are victimized by structures which diminish their rights and freedom. The power and energy of young people is an element in today's world which needs to be taken into account. In countries like Brazil, Venezuela, or India, more than half the population is less than twenty-five years old. What a force for initiative, hope, and enthusiasm is contained in those figures! Within a few years the world will be a world of young people desirous of liberty and equality for all. We are now at a crossroads. Either the adult world manages to understand and win the confidence of the young, giving them their rights and seeking their positive cooperation, or it will find itself faced with an explosion and a dangerous rupture which could lead to continuous confrontation between two forces in need of each other, older people and the young. In other words, a guerrilla war of the most cruel and pervasive sort, since the battlefield will not be one where "outsiders" and the "establishment" clash, but one within the family itself. The resultant explosions will not be less dangerous or harmful because of this "homemade" character.

The atomic explosion is a symbol of our era. It expresses the hope and fear of modern men and women. Yes, the hope. Hope in the possibilities offered by the discovery of such energy, a standing proof that humanity is capable of using any and all means within its reach to achieve its ends.

And fear. For who can guarantee that no nation will unleash an atomic explosion to obtain its political or national ends? Given our experience of humanity, there can never be a guarantee that atomic bombs will not be used so long as they exist in the arsenals of some countries. The only trustworthy guarantee of their nonuse will be their nonexistence.

Our world today finds itself strangely disorientated. It does not know where it is going. It moves along dizzyingly but without any clear direction. What does this hyperactivism seek? What are its objectives? Can anyone answer such questions? Is it to "dominate the world, even the entire cosmos"? How hollow such an answer is when hundreds of millions of people are living a subhuman life. Is it "to obtain a better life"? If so, I must ask: What does "a better life" mean? Do we really wish to reproduce in Asia, Africa, and Latin America "the affluent society," with its frustrations, internal contradictions, wars, and drugs, as well as its material comforts? What kind of person do we seek to educate today? What is the humanism of *homo technicus*?

It surely says a great deal that prominent Hindus are concerned to question whether their government is not aping too slavishly a Western type of economic development at the expense of other fundamental values of a cultural, social, and human nature. Certainly they do not want to turn their backs on technical progress, but neither do they want to see their precious cultural values and religious tradition swallowed up; rather they want to integrate them in a system capable of responding to today's problems.

True though it is that beyond any religious differences they may have, African leaders wish to stop lagging behind economically and technically; it is equally true that they desire to preserve at all costs the values of their several cultures before they are wiped out by a development whose purpose, first and last, is to raise the standard of living in a consumer culture.

Similarly for many Latin American countries, the word "development" is used only with great reservations. What the people saw and experienced of the "Great Society" of the mid-1960s has caused it to lose its attraction and mystique. The "problem-free" life itself becomes *the* great problem by losing its very meaning and, as in some European countries, becoming suicidally hate-ridden.

Nowadays the word "liberation" is much used — liberation of men and women from all exploitation and oppression. This word has wider scope. But what does it mean to be entirely free? And what are the conditions of true freedom?

Even in European and North American countries where economic development has reached its highest level in human history, young people rebel against the comfortable life and the consumer society which their ancestors have built up for them. They react with indifference when invited to contribute to the development of backward countries. They have lost faith in a society, a culture, a type of development which, though it has provided people with much, has at the same time stripped them of important values and created anguishing problems which arouse their indignation.

What is to be done? Useless to indulge in a sterile romanticism and seek to revive a past which is gone, never to return. We must look to the present in function of the past and opening into the future. The past with its rich experience of humanism and transcendental values has taught us a very great deal. The future presents us with a challenge which is difficult but pregnant with great hopes. We must face up to the fundamental problem of our human family in a spirit of total realism.

In the very core of their being, human beings feel an impulse toward good, toward progress. They anxiously seek their own happiness. This is their strongest instinct. Human beings may become persons who lose their way and make gigantic strides in the wrong direction. But the human who pursues evil for the sake of evil does not exist. If people turn to war and violence, it is because they seem to be necessary means for arriving at a truly human, just, and happy society. But is war the remedy for humanity's problems and tensions? Is violence? How can we solve this problem which has troubled humanity since its beginnings? Here we have a fundamental question which torments modern men and women just as it has tormented their forebears.

History shows that neither war nor violent revolution have ever solved our problems; nor will they ever. They are born of hatred and, though hatred harms, it does not heal. It can never be a *human* solution. The new atomic weapons, exponentially increasing our destructive potential for fratricidal conflict, have made us realize how terrible hatred is and have aroused our horror of it. But it is as terrible when it employs the bow, the sling, or the sword as when it makes use of multimegaton atomic bombs. The cancerous cell is as terrible when it is hidden in normal tissue — too minute to be detected by the naked eye — as when, magnified thousands of times under the microscope, its ugliness is revealed. What is deadly and truly terrible about force and violence is not so much their destructive effects as the hatred which spawns them. Hatred, faintly discernible in the struggles of primitive humans, is the same hatred which horrifies us when it is amplified millions of times over in atomic explosions. Neither gunpowder nor dynamite nor atomic power would destroy humanity if there were not hatred. A disease is terrifying so long as it cannot be cured for lack of a proper diagnosis or remedy. A diagnosis of war and violence shows that they are the effects of the virus of hatred. The antidote for hatred is what we call love, and the effect of love is the countersign of war: peace.

In leading us to the central core of matter, atomic physics confronts us with the limits of the material universe. It impels us toward interiority, toward searching for the very root of being and of matter. It is a decisive step inward. When will the day come on which humanity reaches the final stratum of matter and is able to glimpse, as if through a delicate tissue, a new reality encased in all being: the divine reality? Above all, when will we discover that in the core of our person there lives that divine reality? For this we will need a flash of light far more powerful than that which blinded us at Hiroshima: the light of faith which illumines without blinding because it is both powerful and gentle.

On that day, when humans discover, through the light of faith, God — in themselves and in their fellow humans — and see that this God does indeed live and is a God of love, wars and violence will cease and hatred will be no more. God will be seen as the cause of true union and human happiness. On that day will be born a new humanity, that of the children of God.

— "Hiroshima" in *PH* 23–31

VENI, CREATOR SPIRITUS

In 1978, in accordance with the Constitutions *of the Society of Jesus, Arrupe convoked a "Congregation of Procurators," a meeting of elected delegates representing every Jesuit province in the world. The purpose of the Congregation of Procurators was to evaluate the state of the Society three years after the conclusion of General Congregation Thirty-two. In his address that formally closed the Congregation, Father Arrupe concluded with a prayer of supplication to the Holy Spirit. Like his "Prayer to Christ Our Model" (see p. 108) and his "Invocation to the Trinity" (see p. 148), this prayer takes its inspiration from Scripture and from salvation history. Modeled on the well-known Christian prayer of the same name, this version of "Come, Holy Spirit" boldly begs God for the grace to respond to the vocation to which every believer is called by virtue of baptism.*

Lord, I need your Spirit, that divine force that has transformed so many human personalities, making them capable of extraordinary deeds and extraordinary lives. Give me that Spirit which, coming from you and going to you, infinite holiness, is a Holy Spirit.

The judges of Israel, without expecting it, without inclination, without being able to resist, simple sons of villagers, Samson, Gideon, Saul...were changed by you, abruptly and completely. Not only did they become capable of tremendous acts of boldness and strength, but took on new personalities and felt themselves capable of performing a mission as difficult as liberating a whole people. Your action in them was interior, although it is sometimes described by images that emphasize your sudden or strange intervention. You descended upon Samson as a bird of prey and clothed Gideon as with armor.

Feeling the difficulty of my mission, I desire your profound action in my soul, not only that you descend but that you repose in me, and give me those wondrous gifts that you lavish on your elect: wisdom and intelligence, as to Bezalel and Solomon; counsel and strength, as to David; knowledge and fear of God, which was the ideal of so many holy souls of Israel. These gifts will open up for the Society an era of happiness and holiness.

Give me what you gave the Prophets: even if my little being protests, see me forced to speak by a supreme pressure. The word that came to them was not their own word but yours, of your Spirit, sent to them not only to create a new personality for service but also to explain its sense and secrets, of your Spirit that is not only intelligence and strength but also knowledge of God and God's ways. Give me, then, the strength with which you not only opened up to the Prophets your word to the point of revealing to them your glory, but also that strength that kept them standing as they spoke to the people and announced their fate.

With that voice that you make groan in the depths of my being I seek the copious pouring out of yourself, like the rain that gives back life to the arid earth, and like a breath of life that comes to animate dry bones.

Give me that Spirit that scrutinizes all, inspires all, teaches all, that will strengthen me to support what I am not able to support. Give me that Spirit that transformed the weak Galilean fishermen into the columns of your church and into apostles who gave in the holocaust of their lives the supreme testimony of their love for their brothers and sisters.

Thus, this life-giving outpouring will be like a new creation, of hearts transformed, of a sensibility receptive to the voice of the Father, of a spontaneous fidelity to his word. Thus, you will find us again faithful and you will not hide your face from us because you will have poured your Spirit over us. Now I understand that in order to accomplish all this one needs a love like that of the Father, a love that intervenes personally. "You, Lord, are our Father.... Why do you let us stray from your ways?... Oh, that you would tear the heavens open and come down" (Isa. 63:15–19).

Such was your definitive manifestation: the heavens open, a God the Father visible, a God the Son coming down to the earth and becoming human to save the world: "This mystery that has now been revealed through the Spirit to his holy apostles and prophets was unknown to human beings in past generations.... This, then, is what I pray, kneeling before the Father" (Eph. 3:5, 14). *Veni Sancte Spiritus!*

"The one who guarantees these revelations repeats his promise: I shall indeed be with you soon. Amen; come, Lord Jesus. May the grace of the Lord be with you all. Amen" (Rev. 22:20–21).   — "Address to the Procurators" in *SL* 40–42

Epilogue

From Silence, Final Words

Take, O Lord, and receive all my liberty, my memory, my understanding, and my whole will. *Ignatius Loyola*

After suffering a devastating stroke in 1981, Father Arrupe was partially paralyzed and his speech severely impaired. No longer able to physically carry out his duties as Superior General of the Society of Jesus, he sought to resign his office. However, the Society had to wait two years before it could convoke the Thirty-third General Congregation in 1983, at which time it accepted his formal resignation as General and elected his successor, Father Peter Hans Kolvenbach (see Introduction, p. 26).

*The two selections in the Epilogue were written by Father Arrupe and delivered on successive days to the Jesuits gathered at General Congregation Thirty-three. The first, his **Final Address as General of the Society of Jesus**, was read by Father Ignacio Iglesias. Arrupe's address concludes with the famous prayer of St. Ignatius that begins with the words, "Take, O Lord, and receive, all my liberty. . . . " As these words were read, the delegates rose as one and honored their beloved General with a thunderous and prolonged ovation. The second selection, Arrupe's **Final Homily, La Storta, Italy**, was read by Father*

Fernández Castañeda at the mass celebrated by the delegates
the following day in the Chapel at La Storta. Arrupe calls his
remarks his "Nunc Dimittis" (literally, "Now dismiss"), recall-
ing the prayer of the old man Simeon who receives the child
Jesus in the temple with the words, "Now, Master, dismiss your
servant in peace, according to your word, for my eyes have seen
your salvation" (Luke 2:29–30).

FINAL ADDRESS AS GENERAL
OF THE SOCIETY OF JESUS

How I wish I were in a better condition for this meeting with
you! As you see, I cannot even address you directly. But my
General Assistants have grasped what I want to say to everyone.

More than ever, I now find myself in the hands of God. This
is what I have wanted all my life, from my youth. And this is
still the one thing I want. But now there is a difference: the initiative is entirely with God. It is indeed a profound spiritual
experience to know and feel myself so totally in his hands.

At the end of eighteen years as General of the Society, I want
first of all, and above all, to give thanks to the Lord. His generosity toward me has been boundless. For my part, I have tried
to respond, well knowing that all his gifts were for the Society, to be shared with each and every Jesuit. This has been my
persistent effort.

In these eighteen years my one ideal was to serve the Lord
and his church — with all my heart — from beginning to end. I
thank the Lord for the great progress which I have witnessed in
the Society. Obviously, there would be defects too — my own, to
begin with — but it remains a fact that there was great progress,
in personal conversion, in the apostolate, in concern for the

poor, for refugees. And special mention must be made of the attitude of loyalty and filial obedience shown toward the church and the Holy Father, particularly in these last years. For all of this, thanks be to God.

I am especially grateful to my closest collaborators, the General Assistants and Counselors — to Father O'Keefe in the first place — to the Regional Assistants, the whole Curia, and provincials. And I heartily thank Father Dezza and Father Pittau for their loving response to the church and to the Society, on being entrusted with so exceptional a task by the Holy Father.

But above all it is to the Society at large, and to each of my brother Jesuits, that I want to express my gratitude. Had they not been obedient in faith to this poor Superior General, nothing would have been accomplished.

My call to you today is that you be available to the Lord. Let us put God at the center, ever attentive to his voice, ever asking what we can do for his more effective service, and doing it to the best of our ability, with love and perfect detachment. Let us cultivate a very personal awareness of the reality of God.

To each one of you in particular I would love to say — *tantas cosas*: so much, really.

From our young people I ask that they live in the presence of God and grow in holiness, as the best preparation for the future. Let them surrender to the will of God, at once so awesome and so familiar.

With those who are at the peak of their apostolic activity, I plead that they do not burn themselves out. Let them find a proper balance by centering their lives on God, not on their work — with an eye to the needs of the world, and a thought for the millions that do not know God or behave as if they did not. All are called to know and serve God. What a wonderful mission has been entrusted to us: to bring all to the knowledge and love of Christ!

On those of my age I urge openness: let us learn what must be done now, and do it with a will.

To our dear Brothers too, I would like to say *tantas cosas* — so much, and with such affection. I want to remind the whole Society of the importance of the Brothers: they help us to center our vocation on God.

I am full of hope, seeing the Society at the service of the one Lord and of the church, under the Roman Pontiff, the Vicar of Christ on earth. May she keep going along this path, and may God bless us with many and good vocations of priests and Brothers: for this I offer to the Lord what is left of my life, my prayers and the sufferings imposed by my ailments. For myself, all I want is to repeat from the depths of my heart:

Take, O Lord, and receive all my liberty, my memory, my understanding and my whole will.

All I have and all I possess are yours, Lord. You gave them to me and I return them to you. Dispose of them as you will.

Give me your love and your grace, and I shall want for nothing more.   — "A Valediction" in *RR* 173–75

FINAL HOMILY, LA STORTA, ITALY

It is in many ways fitting that at the conclusion of my ministry as Superior General of the Society of Jesus I should come here to La Storta to sing my "Nunc Dimittis" — even though it be in the silence imposed by my present condition.

The veteran Simeon, at the close of a long life of service, and in the magnificent splendor of the Temple of Jerusalem, attained his ardent desire when he received the child Jesus in his arms and drew him to his heart. In the very modest chapel of

La Storta, Ignatius of Loyola, when about to begin a new life of service as founder and first General of our Society, felt himself drawn to the Heart of Christ: "God the Father placed him with Christ his Son," according to his own earnest prayer to the Virgin Mary.

I would not dare compare myself to these two outstanding servants of the Lord. But I can affirm that I have always had a great devotion to the experience of Ignatius at La Storta, and that I am immensely consoled at finding myself in this hallowed place to give thanks to God on arriving at journey's end. "For my eyes have seen your salvation" (Luke 2:20). How often in these eighteen years I have had proof of God's faithfulness to his promise: "I will be favorable to you in Rome."

A profound experience of the loving protection of divine providence has been my strength in bearing the burden of my responsibilities and facing the challenges of our day. True, I have had my difficulties, both big and small. But never has God failed to stand by me. And now more than ever I find myself in the hands of this God who has taken hold of me.

The liturgy of this Sunday seems just made to express my sentiments on this occasion. Like St. Paul I can say that I am "an old man, and now also a prisoner of Christ Jesus" (Philemon 1:9). I had planned things differently, but it is God who disposes, and his designs are a mystery. "Who can divine the will of the Lord?" (see Rom. 11:34). But we do know the will of the Father: that we become true images of the Son. And the Son tells us clearly in the Gospel: "Anyone who does not carry his cross and come after me cannot be my disciple" (Luke 14:27).

Father Laínez, from whom we have the words of the promise, "I will be favorable," proceeds to explain that Ignatius never understood them to mean that he and his companions would be free of suffering. On the contrary, he was convinced that they were called to serve Christ carrying his cross. "He felt he saw

Christ, with the cross on his back, and the eternal Father by his side, saying to him, 'I want you to take this man as your servant.' And so Jesus took him, saying, 'I want you to serve us.' Because of this, conceiving great devotion to this Most Holy Name, he wished to call our fellowship, 'the Society of Jesus.' "

This name had already been chosen by the companions before they came to Rome to offer their services to the pope. But it received a very special confirmation from the experience at La Storta. One can notice a close relationship between the phrases employed by Laínez and those of the Formula of the Institute approved by Julius III: "Whoever wishes to enlist under the standard of the cross as a soldier of God in our Society, which we desire to be distinguished by the name of Jesus, and to serve the Lord alone and the church, his Bride, under the Roman Pontiff, the Vicar of Christ on earth. . . . "

What was for Ignatius the culmination and summing up of so many special graces received since his conversion was for the Society a pledge that it would share in the graces of the founder in the measure in which it remained faithful to the inspiration that gave it birth. I pray that this celebration, that is for me a farewell and a conclusion, be for you and for the whole Society represented here the beginning of a new period of service, with fresh enthusiasm. May the collaboration of the whole Society in the renovation of the chapel of La Storta be an abiding symbol and an unfailing inspiration for a united effort at spiritual renewal, trusting in the graces whose memory is enshrined in La Storta. I shall remain at your side with my prayers.

Like St. Ignatius, I implore the Virgin Mary that we may all be placed with her Son, and that as Queen and Mother of the Society she be with you in all the labors of the General Congregation, and especially in the election of the new General.

— "Father Arrupe's Farewell Homily at La Storta" in *HA* 160–62

Glossary of Ignatian and Jesuit Terms

Ad Majorem Dei Gloriam ("To the Greater Glory of God"): A favorite motto of St. Ignatius. This phrase summarizes the primary purpose of the Society of Jesus. It is often abbreviated *AMDG*. (See also *Magis*.)

Apostolic Orders: The form of religious congregation of which the Society of Jesus is an example. In contrast to monastic orders (e.g., Benedictines) and mendicant orders (e.g., Franciscans, Dominicans), apostolic orders are characterized by their orientation to one or another ministries.

Autobiography of St. Ignatius: Ignatius dictated his spiritual autobiography to Luis Gonçalves de Câmara between 1553 and 1555. It was completed shortly before Ignatius's death.

Call of the Earthly King: An Ignatian Contemplation that appears during the Second Week of the Spiritual Exercises. In this exercise retreatants attend to their desire to be with the Eternal Lord and King, Jesus Christ, serving him and suffering hardships on his behalf.

Cardoner River: The site of the key mystical illumination experienced by Ignatius in 1521 during his time in Manresa. In his *Autobiography* Ignatius states that he saw more in this illumination that in all the other graced experiences of his life put together.

Colloquy / Triple Colloquy: A colloquy is a type of prayer, usually taking the form of spontaneous and familiar conversation directed to a particular personage, such as Christ, the Father, Mary, or one of the saints. In the triple colloquy, retreatants first ask for what they desire through the intercession of Mary, then with her, through the intercession of Christ, and finally, with both Mary and Jesus, the retreatant begs favors directly from God the Father.

Consideration of Different States of Life: A turning point in the Second Week of the Spiritual Exercises. Here retreatants seek indifference to all earthly considerations in order to discern and desire what God wills for them.

Consolation: A spiritual movement that occurs under the action of the Holy Spirit by means of which one is drawn closer to God and through which one experiences an increase in faith, hope, and love. When Ignatius speaks of consolation, he always means "spiritual consolation" — an increase in love for God — as opposed to merely sensual consolation, although genuine spiritual consolation may affect one's senses or emotions.

Constitutions, The: The bylaws of the Society of Jesus, composed by St. Ignatius in his role as the first General of the Society of Jesus.

Contemplation: One of the basic methods of mental prayer for St. Ignatius (along with "meditation"). Contemplation consists in imaginatively gazing upon a particular scene or persons in a Scriptural passage and attending to what the persons say and do.

Contemplation in Action / Contemplative in Action: For St. Ignatius, the ultimate purpose of contemplation (or any spiritual exercise) is to inflame one to love so that one acts on behalf of others and for their good. To be a "contemplative in action" means not only acting "after" contemplating, but acting in such a way that one remains mindful of God's greater glory. This phrase, coined by Nadal to describe Ignatius himself, summarizes the ideal of Ignatian spirituality as a particular path to holiness.

Contemplation for Obtaining Love: This contemplation is the key exercise of the Fourth Week and the climax of the Spiritual Exercises. One considers that every good, including one's life and all one's gifts, comes from God and allows one a share in God's own life and love. Filled with gratitude, one can then respond with Ignatius's famous prayer that begins, "Take, O Lord, and receive all my liberty."

Desolation: A spiritual motion caused by evil spirits that inclines one to move away from God. Ignatius describes as desolation anything that causes "obtuseness of soul, turmoil within it, an impulsive motion toward low and earthly things, or disquiet from various agitations and temptations. These move one toward lack of faith and leave one without hope and without love. One is completely listless, tepid, and unhappy, and feels separated from our Creator and Lord" (*Spiritual Exercises* #317).

Discernment of Spirits: The process by which one attempts to see, recognize, and distinguish spiritual movements caused by the Holy Spirit from those caused by evil spirits, and to detect the nature and source of various consolations and desolations. St. Ignatius provides two sets of "Rules for the Discernment of Spirits" in the Spiritual Exercises.

Discernment of the Will of God: The process whereby one seeks to free oneself from inordinate attachments to worldly desires in order to be able to respond wholeheartedly to the will of God.

Eternal Lord and King / Eternal Lord of All Things: Among St. Ignatius's preferred titles of reverence for Christ or God; he uses the latter to address God in one of the most famous prayers in the *Spiritual Exercises* (#98).

Favre, Pierre: One of the first companions of Ignatius in Paris, the first of the ten companions to be ordained a priest, and one of those present with Ignatius at his famous mystical experience at La Storta.

First Companions: The group of ten friends who met in Paris and formed the Society of Jesus. Led by Ignatius Loyola, they included Francis Xavier, Pierre Favre, Diego Laínez, Alfonso Salmerón, Simão Rodrigues, Nicolás Bobadilla, Claude Jay, Paschase Broët, and Jean Codure.

First Principle and Foundation: The exercise with which the Spiritual Exercises begin. For St. Ignatius, the principle and foundation of any Christian's life is the recognition of the end for which human beings are created, namely, "to praise, reverence, and serve God our Lord, and by means of doing this to save their souls" (*Spiritual Exercises* #23). Analogously, Ignatius and Arrupe speak of the Jesuits' fourth vow of special obedience to the Holy Father as "the principle and foundation" of their religious charism.

Francis Xavier: One of the first companions of Ignatius and among his closest friends. He became a great missionary to India and Japan and died while on his way to China in 1552. He and Ignatius were canonized together in 1622, the first Jesuits to be formally recognized as saints.

General Congregation: A gathering of Jesuits from around the world, representing every province. A congregation includes provincials and elected representatives and represents the highest authority in the Society of Jesus. Congregations are called to elect a new General and to establish priorities for the Society's mission, ministries, and community life.

Gonçalves de Câmara, Luis: A Portuguese Jesuit who entered shortly after the Society was founded; the man to whom Ignatius dictated his autobiography.

St. Ignatius Loyola / Ignatian Spirituality: Pilgrim, mystic, author of the *Spiritual Exercises,* and founder of the Society of Jesus.

Ignatius was born in 1491 in the Basque region of Spain and served as courtier and knight until his conversion in 1521. As the first General of the Society of Jesus, he wrote the *Constitutions*. Ignatius died in Rome in 1556 and was canonized in 1622. "Ignatian spirituality" designates the highly original spiritual path that he mapped out in the light of his own mystical experiences.

Illumination: A mystical experience, like that which St. Ignatius experienced at the Cardoner River, and which (in contrast to a "vision") involves having "the eyes of one's understanding" opened.

Indifference: The technical Ignatian term for the grace of genuine inner freedom in the face of any decision. Ignatian indifference has nothing to do with apathy or a lack of concern; rather, it has to do with freedom from inordinate attachments.

Inordinate Attachment: For St. Ignatius, any affection, inclination, urge, like, or dislike that tends to lead one away from the will of God, the true good of one's life.

Janssens, Jean-Baptiste: Arrupe's immediate predecessor as Superior General of the Society of Jesus. He served from 1946 to 1964.

Jerusalem: The site of St. Ignatius's first pilgrimage in 1522 and the intended goal of the first companions in 1538. When they were unable to go to Jerusalem, Ignatius and his companions placed themselves at the service of the pope and soon thereafter formed the Society of Jesus.

Laínez, Diego: One of the first companions of Ignatius in Paris and one of the most important figures in the early Society of Jesus. He and Pierre Favre were with Ignatius at La Storta; it is Laínez who provided most of the important details about that foundational mystical experience. Along with Jerónimo Nadal, he is credited with convincing Ignatius to dictate his *Autobiography*.

He succeeded Ignatius as the second General of the Society of Jesus.

La Storta: The site of one of the most important mystical experiences of Ignatius's life while on the way to Rome in 1537. In it Ignatius "saw the Father place him with His Son." On the basis of this experience Ignatius insisted that the company he and his companions founded take the name of Jesus.

Magis: Latin for "greater good." The *magis* provides criteria for spiritual discernment when one must make a choice between two goods. It functions as a short form of the Latin motto *Ad Majorem Dei Gloriam.*

Manresa: The site of the cave where Ignatius stayed in 1522–23. During this time Ignatius engaged in a number of ascetical and spiritual practices. He grew in his understanding of the discernment of spirits and experienced numerous mystical graces, including the illumination at the Cardoner River. His experiences at Manresa formed the germ of his *Spiritual Exercises.*

Monserrat: Site where Ignatius held an all-night vigil on March 24, 1522. Prior to setting out on the pilgrimage that would take him to Manresa and eventually to Jerusalem, Ignatius fasted for three days and then held a vigil before the statue of the Madonna in the Church of Our Lady of Monserrat.

Nadal, Jerónimo: One of chief assistants of Ignatius in Rome, along with Juan de Polanco and Diego Laínez. Much of our information about Ignatius comes from Nadal. He is also among the most important early commentators on the Spiritual Exercises.

Pamplona: The site where Ignatius was seriously wounded by a cannonball while helping defend a fortress near the city. During his long convalescence from this injury Ignatius underwent a spiritual conversion. Hence, the name "Pamplona" is often associated with Ignatius's conversion.

Paris: Between 1528 and 1535, Ignatius lived in Paris and took up theology studies at the University of Paris. It was here that the first companions met one another and were directed by Ignatius in the Spiritual Exercises. Together they founded the Society of Jesus.

Paul III, Pope: The pope who officially founded the Society of Jesus in 1540 and gave a formal approbation to the *Spiritual Exercises* in 1548, when the first print edition was published.

Pilgrim: The name Ignatius uses to refer to himself in his *Autobiography.* It functions as a symbol for Ignatius's way of thinking about his own life in the world; as such, "to be a pilgrim" is a key part of the Jesuit ideal.

Polanco, Juan de: One of chief assistants of Ignatius in Rome, along with Jerónimo Nadal and Diego Laínez.

Province / Provincial: The "province" represents the basic administrative unit of the Society of Jesus; the "provincial" is the Jesuit Superior appointed by the General to oversee the ordinary governance of a Jesuit province.

Retreat / Thirty-Day Retreat: In Ignatian spirituality, a period of time set aside to make the Spiritual Exercises. The basic form of Exercises is a "thirty-day retreat," although it can be adapted to an eight-day format as well as many other formats.

Ribadeneira, Pedro de: An early Jesuit, he joined the order in 1540 at the age of fourteen. He had a close relationship with Ignatius and wrote the first biography of him in 1572.

Santa Maria della Strada: The first church held by the Society of Jesus. The Church of the Gesù, the mother church of the Society, presently stands on the site.

Society of Jesus / Jesuit Order / Our Least Society: The religious order founded by St. Ignatius and the First Companions with the approval of Pope Paul III in 1540. Ignatius liked to refer to the order as "our least Society."

Souls / Good of Souls: Ignatius frequently uses the word "souls" to mean "the whole person." The "good of souls" is anything that helps others respond to the grace of salvation (the ultimate good of all persons and thus, in Ignatius's view, the principle and foundation of every human being's life).

Spiritual Direction: The activity by which one person, usually one with experience in the spiritual life, gives assistance to another by proposing exercises for prayer and by helping with the discernment of spiritual motions.

Spiritual Exercises: The detailed method of spirituality developed by St. Ignatius on the basis of his mystical experiences at Manresa, and the foundation of Ignatian spirituality and Jesuit formation.

Spiritual Movements / Motions: A technical term used by Ignatius to designate a variety of interior experiences. Examples of motions include thoughts, feelings, impulses, inclinations, moods, temptations, consolations, desolations, and the like. They may arise as a result of the action of good or evil spirits, or they may arise from human nature and appear more or less neutral.

Three Classes of Human Beings / Third Class of Human Beings: The "Three Classes of Human Beings" is an original Ignatian meditation from the Second Week of the Spiritual Exercises. It follows the meditation on the "Two Standards" and proposes three types of person differentiated by varying degrees of spiritual freedom: those who put off the challenge; those who seek to compromise with the challenge; and the "third class of human beings," those who seek and achieve genuine spiritual freedom or indifference.

Three Degrees of Humility / Third Degree of Humility: The "Three Degrees of Humility" is a meditation from the Second Week of the Spiritual Exercises. It represents one of Ignatius's

most important and original meditations. The three degrees are proposed in ascending order of perfection. In praying for the "third degree of humility," one goes beyond indifference to poverty, for example, and actually "desires and chooses poverty with Christ poor."

Two Standards / Standard of Christ / Standard of the Cross / Standard of Satan: The "Two Standards" meditation from early in the Second Week of the Spiritual Exercises is among the most important and original meditations proposed by Ignatius. The image of a "standard" corresponds to a banner or flag that an army might take into battle to indicate its allegiance. In this exercise, Ignatius juxtaposes the "standard of Satan" and the "standard of Christ" (alternately referred to as the "standard of the Cross.")

Weeks of the Spiritual Exercises: The Ignatian term for the four units or sections of the Spiritual Exercises. When one is making a thirty-day retreat, each unit may run for approximately one week (although in actual practice, the temporal duration is unimportant.) The weeks are distinguished by the primary themes over which one meditates and the graces for which one prays. The exercises of the "First Week" attend to the reality of sin against the backdrop of God's love and mercy. The "Second Week" focuses primarily on the following of Jesus and the choice of how one will live one's life. The "Third Week" focuses on the passion of Jesus and the "Fourth Week" on the resurrection.